PHRASAL VERB FUN

Peter Gray

Second Edition, Enlarged and Revised

No part of this book may be reproduced, scanned, or distributed in any printed or electronic form without permission. Please do not participate in or encourage piracy of copyrighted materials in violation of the author's rights.

Copyright 2014 © Peter Gray

For the second edition, I want to thank four people in particular who helped me; Noni Lu, may there be no end to our friendship; José Sierra, who now knows when something is broken or not quite right; Missy Issy, who <u>insisted</u> on paper pages; and MªJesús Segura for being such a fantastic friend.

This book is dedicated to all my students who taught me most of what I know

How to use this book

Most people think that phrasal verbs, verbs with more than one word, are hard to learn. As students we are given lists and lists of them to memorise, and we usually find the whole thing boring, complicated, and really hard to remember.

This book is different. There are no lists and there is nothing to memorise. Instead, there are over 600 little stories, one for each verb. The fact is that phrasal verbs are not a logical system, designed by some maniac a few centuries ago. No. There are simply something that grew up naturally.

Most natives don't even know the expression phrasal verbs. We never learn them at school. We know the difference between chopping down a tree and then chopping it up. We also know that when a building burns down, it is the same as when it burns up. Neither do we ever confuse put up your cousin with put up with him.

When I was thinking about this book, I quickly discovered that the verbs fell into groups, and that the up of drink up had a completely different meaning from the up of give up. So I grouped these verbs together in the particle index on page 25. You might like to go there first.

I suggest that you start anywhere you like in this book, and then jump about at random for about ten minutes. Don't try to memorise, don't try to learn. Just play with it. You may like to say the various sentences aloud. You may like to pretend to be a star and speak in front of your bathroom mirror as to an adoring crowd. Be an actor. Fool around. Have fun with it.

Then next day, another ten minutes.

If you do this every day, I money-back guarantee that in about ten days you will know more about phrasal verbs than 99% of all non-native teachers who teach English for a living.

I also promise you that you will have fun doing it.

By the way, if you are lucky enough to live in Zaragoza, in Spain, then you may want to come and say hello some evenings.

ZaragozaConversation.com for more.

Phrasal Verb Structure

Phrasal verbs are verbs with more than one word.

There are four categories - from the point of view of structure - and you must be clear which category each verb belongs to.

1. Two-word verb without an object, sometimes called intransitive verbs (because the action is not 'transmitted' to an object).

For example

Every morning, I get up. (No object. Nobody else is involved.)

No problem.

2a. Inseparable two-word verb This means that nothing can go between the two words.

That horrible dog just turned on me. (It suddenly attacked me.)

This is not a problem if you learn this verb as *turn on me, turn on you, turn on him*, and so on.

2b. Separable two-word verb This can be a little more difficult. If the object is short, like a pronoun (you remember, words like *I, me, him, us*) it *MUST* come between the two words of the verb. If not, you have a choice.

For example

I turned on the television.
I turned the television on.
I turned it on. (Now we can watch it.)

This can be a problem. So you have to remember it as *turn it on*.

3. Three-word verbs are almost always inseparable.

I don't know how you put up with him. He is so rude all the time.

No problem.

But there is a small group of three-word verbs which have an object

<u>get it over with</u>
<u>put it down to</u>
<u>take it up with</u>

Verb Index

ask
ask about
ask after
ask around
ask out

be
be about to
be for
be in for
be on for
be up for
be into
be off
be over
be round
be to
be up to

back
back down
back off
back out
back up

bang
bang on
bang on about
bang up

bank
bank on
bear
bear down
bear down on
bear out
bear up
bear up under
bear with
beat
beat up
boil
boil down to
blow
blow away
blow out
blow over
blow up
bottle
bottle out
break
break away
break down
break in, break into
break off
break out, break out of
break out in

break through
break up
break up with
bring
bring about
bring down
bring off
bring out
bring round
bring up
brush
brush off
brush up
burn
burn down
burn out
burn up
call
call after
call by
call for
call off
call out
call out (call sb out on sth)
call round
call to
call up
calm

calm down
carry
get carried away
carry off
carry on
carry on with
carry out
catch
catch on
catch on to
catch out
catch up
catch up with
chat
chat up
cheer
cheer up
check
check in
check out
check up on
close
close down
come
come about
come across
come across something

come across with
come after
come apart
come at
come between
come by
come by something
come down to
come down with
come forward
come in for
come into
come off
come on
come out
come out in
come out with
come round
come to, come round to
come under
come up against
come up to
come up with
count
count down
count in (count me in)
count on
cross

cross out
cut
cut back
cut back on
cut down
cut down on
cut in
cut off
cut out
cut up
deal
deal in
deal out
deal with
die
die away
die down
die off
die out
do
do away with
do in
do up
do with (I could do with that)
do without
dress
dress up

drink
drink up
drop
drop back
drop by
drop in, drop in on
drop off
drop out
drop round
dry
dry out
dry up
end
end up
face
face up to
fall
fall about
fall apart
fall away
fall back
fall back on
fall behind
fall behind with
fall down
fall for
fall in

fall in with
fall off
fall on
fall out, fall out with
fall over
fall through
fall under
feel
feel down
feel up to
figure
figure out
fill
fill in, fill out
fill up
find
find out
fit
fit in
fix
fix up
follow
follow through
follow up
get
get about, get around
get across

get ahead
get along
get around
get at
get away with
get back at
get back into
get behind
get by
get down to
get into
get off
get off on
get off with
get on
get out
get out of (what do you get out of it?)
get over
get over it
get it over
get it over with
get round
get round to
get through
get through, get through to
get up

give
give away
give in

give off
give out
give up
give somebody up
give way

go
go after
go at
go ahead
go away
go back on
go down (well)
go down with
go for
go in for
go in with
go off
go on
go on about
go on for
go out
go out with
go over
go through
go through with
go under
go up against
go with
go without

grow
grow apart
grow out of
grow up
hand
hand down
hand out
hand over
hang
hang on
hang up
have
have on (have me on)
hold
hold against
hold down (a job)
hold on
hold out, hold out for
hold up
join
join in
join up
keep
keep ahead
keep at
keep in with
keep off

keep on
keep on about
keep out
keep up,
keep up with
knock
knock about
knock off
knock out
know
know about
know of
lay
lay off
lay out
leave
leave out
let
let down
let off
lie
lie down
lie in
live
live it down
live off
live together

live it up
live up to
live with
look
look about
look after
look ahead
look around
look back
look back at
look back on
look back to
look down on
look for
look forward to
look into
look out
look out for
look over
look round
look through
look up
look up to
make
make for
make out
make up
make it up to you

make up for
make up to
mix
mix up
move
move in
move off
move out
move over
move to
move up
name
name after
name for
own
own up to
pass
pass away
pass down
pass for
pass off
pass on
pass out
pass over
pass up
pick
pick off

pick on
pick out
pick up
pick up on
play
play at
play back
play down
play up
point
point out
pull
pull ahead
pull away
pull back
pull off
pull through
push
push ahead
push around
push for
push off
put
put about
put across
put aside
put away
put by

put down
put it down to
put forward
put off
put on
put out
put over
put through
put up
put up with
put upon
rule
rule out
run
run across
run away
run down
run for
run into
run out
run out of
run over
run through
run up
see
see about
see in
see off

see out
see it through
see through it
see to
sell
sell by
sell off
sell out
sell up
send
send back
send down
send up
set
set about
set after
set against
set aside
set back
set down
set forward
set in
set off
set on
set out (on a journey)
set out (things on a table)
set up
settle

settle for
show
show off
show up
shut
shut up
sign
sign on
sign up
sink
sink in
sit
sit down
sit up
sort
sort out
split
split away
split off
split up
speak
speak out
speak up
start
start out
start up

stand
stand by
stand for (public office)
stand for (something with meaning)
stand in for
stand out
stand up for
stand up to

stay
stay ahead
stay off
stay out
stay up

step
step down
step up to

stick
stick at
stick by
stick to
stick up for
stick up to
stick with

take
take after
take away
take back
take down

take for
take from (take it from me)
take in
take off
take on
take out
take over
take to
take up
take up with (take it up with him)
talk
talk around
talk back
talk down to
talk over
talk round
talk somebody round
tell
tell off
think
think about
think back
think of
think over
think through
think up
throw
throw away

throw out
throw up
try
try for
try on
try out
turn
turn about
turn against
turn around
turn away
turn down
turn in
turn in (turn him in)
turn into
turn off
turn on
turn on (somebody)
turn out
turn over
turn round
turn to
turn up
use
use up
watch
watch for
watch out

watch out for
watch over
wear
wear in
wear out
work
work off
work on
work out
work round to

Particle Index

about

About has several meanings: one of the most common meanings is moving from here to there to somewhere else. For example; 'Veronica ran about the village all morning.' means that she went from house to shop to church to who-knows-where all morning.

Sometimes but not always around and round have the same meaning.

ask about, ask around
fall about
get about, get around, get round
knock about
look about, look around, look round
put about
turn about, turn around, turn round

Another meaning is 'near here' in space or 'almost now' in time.
For example -
be about to
bring about
come about

about

What was that film about? What was its theme?
see about
set about

after

Usually, this means later in time
call after

come after
go after
name after
set after
take after

---

ask after
look after

against

Against always has the idea of *'confrontation'*. It is never friendly. To be against something means that you don't like it, that you disagree with it.

come up against
go up against
hold against
set against
turn against

ahead

In any race, the one who is winning, is *ahead*. It is the direction where you are going.

get ahead
go ahead
keep ahead
look ahead
pull ahead
push ahead
stay ahead

around

Around has two main meanings. The most common meaning is vaguely moving from one direction to another. What do many people do on holiday? They walk around the town where they are staying. About and round mean the same, and several verbs have all three forms which mean the same..

The second meaning of *around* and *about* is approximate.

How much is it? About ten euros. It is around ten euros.

ask around, ask round, ask about
fall about
get around, get round, get about
knock about, knock around
look around, look round, look about
push around
put around, put about
talk around, talk round
turn around, turn round, turn about

at

At is static. It means two things together, the same time. To be in contact.

We sit *at* the table - the normal position for eating or working. We arrive *at* a small place like a railway station (although we arrive *in* a big place like China). Jack and Jill work *at* the same place, and they both finish work *at* six o'clock.

At is frequently more aggressive than *to*

For example, if you shout *at* people, you are being abusive. But if you shout *to* somebody across the street, you are saying hello.

If you talk or speak *at* your friends, you are being very boring - talking, talking, talking, and not listening. But if you speak or talk *to* them, that is normal conversation.

Compare come at with come to and point to

with point at
get at
get back at
go at
keep at
stick at

away

Away means you never see it again
blow away
break away
die away
fall away
get carried away
do away with
get away
get away with
give away
go away
pass away
pull away
put away
run away
split away
take away
throw away
turn away
Although, *put away* is not always permanent

back

Back, after a verb, nearly always has the sense of *'return'*
cut back
fall back on
get back at
get back into

go back
go back on
look back
look back at
look back on
look back to
play back
pull back
send back
take back
talk back
think back

back

Often, *back* means the opposite of forward
drop back
fall back
set back

by

In space, *by* has the general idea of *'next to'* or *'close to'*
call by
come by
drop by
get by
put by
stand by
stick by

by

By in time means *'at or before'*
The court case is on 12th June. All the papers have to be submitted by that date.
sell by

down

The direction towards the earth is *down*. By extension, it can mean a depressing or sad mood, or even just the end of euphoria. It means less intensity and with a series of numbers it means in the direction back to zero.

bear down
bear down on
bring down
burn down
calm down
close down
come down with
count down
cut down
die down
feel down
go down (well)
go down with
let down
lie down
live it down
play down
run down
set down
sit down
take down
turn down

down

Down also has a social meaning. It means something like *'socially inferior'*. Snobs, people who think they are superior, are very sensitive to this.

back down
look down on

put down
send down
step down

down

Down is real, here and now. *Up* is the world of fantasy and imagination. *'Down to earth'* is a common way of saying this. The opposite, a dreamer, is *'up in the clouds'*.
calm down
come down to
break down
get down to
hold down

down

Often we imagine a calendar that has the past written at the top and then it goes *down* to the present day.
hand down
pass down

down

Down also has the meaning of *'reduce'*
boil down to
break it down
cut down

for

For is often a purpose. It is the reason why you do something.
be for
be in for
be on for

be up for
call for
go for
go in for
look for
look out for
make up for
push for
run for
stand for
stand up for
try for
watch for
watch out for

for

For can sometimes indicate that one thing or person can be instead of, or in the place of, a second one.

name for
pass for
settle for
stand in for
take for

for

I did it *for* you. I did it *for* your benefit. The opposite of *against*.

stand up for
stick up for

forward

The direction in which we are going (most of the time) is *forward*.

come forward

look forward to
put forward
set forward

in

Static or dynamic, *in* usually means what the dictionary says. That means you can *'be in'* a room and you are not moving. You can also *'go in'* the bathroom.

be in for
break in
break out in
check in
come in to
count (somebody) in
cut in
deal in
drop in
drop in on
fall in
fall in with
fill in
fit in
give in
go in for
go in with
join in
keep in with
lie in
move in
see in
sink in
take in
turn in
turn sb in

in

In can also mean around here, now - the opposite of out there
set in

off

Off often has the sense of being away from the target, the intention, what is right, separation. Something not right.
be off
break off
call off
cut off
fall off
give off
go off (like bad food)
go off (somebody or something)
knock off
lay off
let off
live off
pass off
put off
sell off
show off
split off
tell off

off

Off can sometimes mean *'away from here'*
back off
be off (starting a journey)
carry off
get off with
go off (on a journey)

move off
see off
set off (on a journey)

off

Off can also mean a change of state or position
bring off
come off
go off (like old milk)
pick off
pull off
push off
set off (a firework)
take off (from an airport)

off

Off is also the opposite of *on*, or it can be a move away from an *on* position.
drop off
get off, get off on
keep off
stay off
turn off (the computer)
work off (all that fat that was ON you)

on

On, 'on top of', literally means the position above something that touches that thing.
My dinner is on the plate. The plate is on the table.
bear down on
put on
sign on
try on

There can be something solid and stable about *on*.
count on
take on
work on
And sometimes it is aggressive.
fall on
pick on
set on
turn on (somebody)

on

We often use *on* to mean 'continue'
bang on
carry on
carry on with
get on ('How are you getting on?')
go on
go on for
hang on
hold on
keep on
keep on about
pass on
take on

on

On is the opposite of *off*
be on for
turn on (the computer)

out

Out is the opposite of *in*. It can also mean *'going from inside' out* in the world.
ask out

back out
break out (disease)
break out in
bring out
call out
call sb out on sth
come out
come out in
come out with
cut out
drop out
find out
get out
get out of (What do you get out of it?)
go out with
move out
pick out
run out, run out of
set out
speak out
stand out
stay out
throw out
try out
work out

out

Out can mean 'extent', 'away from here' 'not here but everywhere'
bottle out
dry out
fill out
give out
hand out
lay out
look out

pass out
point out
set out
start out
watch out
watch out for

out

The final result, the conclusion, the end.
bear out
carry out
catch out
die out
figure out
knock out
see out
sort out
turn out
wear out
work out (a problem)

out

Another meaning is to exclude
cross out
deal out
leave out
rule out

out

Out is when a fire stops burning. We feel cold then, just as we do when we go outside. It has the sense of *'no more'*.
blow out
burn out
cross out

go out
put out
rule out

out

With your chest out in pride
hold out

over

Over often means 'from one side to the other'
get over
hand over
move over
pass over
put over
talk over
think over
turn over

over

Over can have the sense of 'finished', 'complete' or 'we don't have to think about it any more'
be over
blow over
get over it
get it over with

over

Over sometimes means seeing things from above or from a distance. You deal with the big picture but not the details. In other words, you can see the forest but not the trees. It can be the opposite of *under*.
go over

look over
take over
watch over

round

Round means the same as *around* and *about* in the sense of here and there and everywhere.
ask round, ask around, ask about
be round
come round
drop round
get round, get around, get about
get round him
look round, look around, look about
talk somebody round
turn around, turn round, turn about
But notice that *round* does **not** mean approximate.

through

Through means movement from *outside* of something, *in* to it, and then *outside* it again.
A train goes through a tunnel.
Light goes through the stained-glass window.
The pilgrims went through the dark, dark wood.
But
We go over a bridge, or across a river.
break through
fall through
follow through
get through it
get through, get through to
go through
go through with
look through

pull through
put through
run through
see (it) through
see through (it)
think through

to

To is often more friendly than *on* or *at*.
turn to
If you shout *to* somebody across the street, you are saying hello, but if you shout *at* them, you are being abusive.
If you speak or talk *to* your friends, that is normal conversation, but if you talk or speak *at* them, you are being very boring - talking, talking, talking, and not listening.
Notice that we listen *to* people, which is polite, but we look *at* them which may not be polite at all.
Compare come to with come at, and point to with point at.

under

The opposite of *over*
come under
fall under
go under

up

Up often has the sense of completing or finishing something.
beat up
break up
bring up (your children)

burn up
check up on
cut up
drink up
dry up
end up
fill up
follow up
grow up
mix up
sell up
shut up
split up
use up

It can also have the related idea of reaching a limit.

bang up
catch up, catch up with
come up against
come up to
go up against
move up
step up to

up

The direction away from earth is *up*. It can also mean increasing intensity.

be up to
bear up
blow up
bring up (your food)
face up to
get up
look up
pick up
pick up on

play up
put up
put up with
run up
set up
show up
show (somebody) up
sit up
speak up
stand up for
stand up to
stick up for
stick up to
take up
think up
throw up
turn up
turn up (the music)

up

This *up* is the direction of Heaven and authority. This is not *up* in the scientific physical sense.

call up
give up
give somebody up
join up
own up to
pass up
sign up
take it up with

up

This *up* is social, and means high social class.

look up to
make up to

up
Up is a higher standard than before
brush up
do up
dress up
fix up
live up to
make up
make up for

up
Up is the world of fantasy and imagination, of feeling better. *Down* is real, here and now.
chat up
cheer up
feel up to
live it up
start up

Verbs

ask
(ask, asked, asked)

When you use your voice to <u>find out</u> new information. You ask questions. You ask people questions. Once you asked your mother, 'Why is the sky blue?'

ask about, ask around

Maybe you want to know which restaurant in your town is the best for a celebration, so you ask all your friends. You ask around all your friends. You ask around.
Ask about has the same meaning.
<u>Two-word verb without an object</u> *No problem.*

BUT to *ask about something* means something different.
Mrs Omicron asked me about my new job. Did I like it?

ask after

In the morning I saw Jenny. I asked her, 'How is your sister, Jenny?' I asked after her sister. This <u>after</u> is similar to <u>look after</u>.
<u>Inseparable two-word verb</u> *No problem.*

ask out

When you ask somebody <u>out</u>, it is romantic. It means that you hope to <u>go out with</u> them.

'Philomena, would you like to come and play bingo with me on Thursday night? We could have a beer afterwards.'
Peregrine has just asked Philomena out.
<u>Separable two-word verb</u> *Be careful.*

back
(back, backed, backed)
Your back is the part of the body that is away from the direction you normally move. It's the same for a car or a train. It is, of course, the most dangerous place an attack can come from. The verb *to back* has two main senses. To move in the opposite direction from normal, or to help protect someone else from an attack from his back, to add your forces to theirs.

When a sponsor or an investor gives you money so you can <u>keep on</u> with your work, they are backing you.

back down
<u>Down</u> is the socially bad place to be. (Think of <u>look down on</u> or <u>put down</u>) When someone *backs down* from a confrontation, he has lost. He did not have enough courage to dominate. He submitted to the strength of the other. No Hollywood Hero ever backs down.
<u>Two-word verb without an object</u> *No problem.*

back off

You are going for a walk in the jungle when suddenly you see a large snake on the path. What do you do? You *back off*. You go back the way you came. You retreat. This off means 'away from here'.
Two-word verb without an object No problem.

back out

This *out* means 'coming from inside' out in the world. Literally, you can back your car out of your garage. So, by extension, you can back out of a situation.

LongShot Corporation was about to make a good offer for the ForgetMeNot Company, but they backed out at the last minute.

They decided not to go ahead with it.
Notice that unlike back down or back off there is no sense of danger or fear here.
Two-word verb without an object No problem.

back up

When you back something or somebody up, you are reinforcing them and making them stronger. When you back up your friend, you are helping him against his enemies. When you back up what he says, you are giving more evidence that what he says is true. And when you back up the files in your computer, you are making extra copies in case of disaster.
Separable two-word verb Be careful.

bang
(bang, banged, banged)
This is not usually a verb on its own. A bang is any loud sudden noise.

bang on, bang on about
This is an impolite way of describing somebody who is talking, talking, talking about something so boring that you stopped listening a long ago. This <u>on</u> means 'continue' like <u>go on</u> or <u>carry on</u>.
'Oh,dear,' said Spoiled Suzy. 'That was my dad on the phone. He is always banging on about me being late home at night.'
BANG ON <u>Two-word verb without an object</u> No problem
BANG ON ABOUT <u>Three-word verb</u> No problem.

bang up
I haven't had the experience myself, but I have heard that you never forget the bang of the prison gate when it closes behind you as you go in. Up often means the end. When you are banged <u>up</u> you are not going anywhere for a long time.
Usually this is passive.
Charlie the Coker was banged up for fifteen years.
<u>Two-word verb without an object</u> No problem.

bank
(bank, banked, banked)
Not usually a verb, but sometimes we say, 'You can bank it.' meaning 'You can put it in

the bank.'

bank on

In the old days, we used to think that banks were safe places for our money. 'You can bank on it.' means that something is as secure as your money in a bank.
'Will Henrietta come to work tomorrow?'
'Yes. You can bank on it.'
It's sure. It is certain. Henrietta will definitely be coming to work tomorrow.
<u>Inseparable two-word verb</u> No problem.

bear

(bear, bore, born.
Like *tear, tore, torn* and *wear, wore, worn*)
Literally *bear* means to support. A load-bearing wall is a wall in a building that takes the weight. If you knock out a load-bearing wall, the building will collapse. A component in a machine could be a stress-bearing component. It is designed to be strong enough to bear the stress.
Sometimes when the horrible music goes on too long, we say, 'I can't bear it.'

bear down, bear down on

A load bearing <u>down</u> on you could be a great weight of worry. Anything that feels heavy that you cannot avoid, such as a large debt, could bear down on you. This <u>on</u>, of course, means *on top of*. The debt is on top of you.
BEAR DOWN <u>Inseparable two-word verb</u> No problem.
BEAR DOWN ON <u>Three-word verb</u> No problem.

bear out

The facts don't bear out your story. In other words, you story is not supported by any facts. This <u>out</u> means the conclusion. We conclude that the evidence doesn't bear out your story, therefore you're lying to the court.
<u>Separable two-word verb</u> Be careful.

bear up, bear up under

'How are you today?'
'Bearing up.'
This means that our friend has problems <u>bearing down on</u> him, but he is still standing tall. He is bearing <u>up</u>. He is bearing up under the strain.
BEAR UP <u>Two-word verb without an object</u> No problem.
BEAR UP UNDER <u>Three-word verb</u> No problem.

bear with

I know I am talking too much, but I have something important to say. Have a little patience, be strong, bear with me.
<u>Inseparable two-word verb</u> No problem.

be

The most irregular verb in the English language.
In the present
I am
you are
he is
she is

it is
we are
you are
they are
It is the only verb with more than one form in the past
I was
you were
he was
she was
it was
we were
you were
they were
The past participle is *been*

be about to

Mrs Cornell was about to sign the agreement, when her lawyer rushed into the room, and stopped her just in time. In a few seconds she would have made an expensive mistake.

About has several meanings. One of these meanings is *near here* in space, or *almost now* in time.

So, if I *am about to* buy you a drink, it means that I am going to buy you that drink in the very near future.

Three-word verb *No problem.*

be for, be in for, be on for, be up for

One of the commonest meanings of for is a

purpose. It is the reason why you do something.

Imagine an old-fashioned union meeting where democracy was always with a show of hands. There were only two possible positions for industrial action. You were <u>for</u> it, or you were <u>against</u> it. You were in favour of the strike or not. That means, you wanted it or you did not.

Like music, language has variations on a theme. There is usually more than one way to express yourself.

I'm in for it, means I'*m in* the group of people who are *for* this action.

For example, we are a band of thieves. Shall we rob the big bank next Friday when it has the most cash? Yes, we decide, we *are in for* it.

We could also say, Yes we'*re on for* it. The robbery is <u>on</u>. It has not been <u>called off</u>.

Yes, we might say, we'*re up for* it. This has the suggestion that we have the courage to say yes.

BE FOR is an <u>Inseparable two-word verb</u> *No problem.*
BE IN FOR, BE ON FOR, BE UP FOR are <u>three-word verbs</u>. *No problems, either.*

be into

Julian hated the idea of studying Canadian interest-rate policy, but he gradually <u>got into</u> it, and now he has become an expert.
Now he *is into* it.

Quite recent, I think. If something is very very interesting, if it takes all your attention, you have the feeling that you are inside it, that it is all around you. To *be into* an idea or an interest, or to get into it, is to be absorbed by it, to be fascinated by it.

Notice something strange about this verb. *Into*, except here, always shows movement. We can *go into* a room, or we can *get into* a car. These are movements. They take time. Then we are *in* the room or the car. And we could stay there forever.
To BE INTO is only used as an enthusiasm, never as a physical fact.
<u>Inseparable two-word verb</u> No problem.

be off

The Baron was a terrible shot. He was always off the target. He never hit a grouse all day.
This milk's off! (It's not right. It smells bad. It <u>has gone off</u>)
We often use <u>off</u> to mean being away from the target, or the intention.
Mr Hendricks wanted to be a millionaire before he was thirty. He was off by four years.
(He had to wait until he was thirty-four.)
The show *is off*. It has been cancelled. (It has been <u>called off</u>.)

We sometimes say <u>off</u> for 'away from here'.
To be off, as in *'I'm off now!'* (I'm going away now)
This is the same as *'I'm <u>going off</u> now!'*

'I'm <u>setting off</u> now!' is very similar, but has the suggestion of a longer journey. You might say this if you were leaving to start a new job in another country.

And *'Be off with you!'* is what we say to a child when we want them to go away.

<u>Two-word verb without an object</u> No problem.

be over

(1) 'I'll *be over* in the morning' means almost exactly the same as *'I'll be round in the morning'* but it is slightly more business-like. It sounds as though the speaker is on business. The image is that I will have succeeded in getting over all the obstacles in the street on the way to your office.

(2) *'It's all over now, Baby Blue,'* sang Bob Dylan. It's all finished. It will never happen again. This <u>over</u> means complete, finished, the end.

<u>Two-word verb without an object</u> No problem.

be round

'I'll be round in the morning' means almost exactly the same as *'I'll be over in the morning'* but it is slightly more casual. As in many verbs, <u>round</u> means *'approximately here'* or *'here, but not urgently'*. *'Come to my house'* is direct and businesslike, but *'come round to my house'* is friendly and more relaxed.

<u>Two-word verb without an object</u>. No problem.

be to

We are at the end of a business meeting, and many things have been decided. Charles is to write a report for the managing director, Elena is to recruit the five new people that the project needs, and the managing director, Mr Harare, is to meet everybody else again in a week.

This means that everything has been decided.

Mary is to go to London on Tuesday.

(This is definitely formal and business-like. It implies that Mary has accepted the responsibility of going to London.)

<u>Inseparable two-word verb</u> No problem.

be up to

'What are you up to?' we ask a child. It means the same as *'What are you doing right now?'* When a little child is lying down, usually there is no problem. But if children are <u>up</u>, there is a big chance that they are up to mischief, that they are doing something that they should not be doing, that they are being naughty. So -

'What are you up to?' means *'What are you doing? Are you being naughty? Are you causing trouble?'*

<u>Three-word verb</u> No problem.

beat

(beat, beat, beaten)

means to strike, to hit or exceed in

competition

beat up

Alan was an aggressive boy who loved beating up his classmates. Later, he became a football hooligan.

Often, up has the sense of completing or finishing a job. Remember fill up a bottle, which means *'fill it to the top'*, drink up and so on.

Beating up is what some people do to other people when they don't like them. They beat them so much that their victims don't ever want to be beaten again. Thugs particularly like this verb. They beat people up for fun.

Separable two-word verb Be careful.

blow
(blow, blew, blown)
What the wind does.

blow away

When the wind blows something away, we never see it again. This is also what happens when somebody gets murdered. We never see them again. Films tell us that this is how gangsters refer to their victims. They get *blown away*. That is, they get murdered. They disappear.

Separable two-word verb Be careful.

blow out

When a fire dies, it goes out. Maybe it is

because we feel that the heat of the fire has gone out of the room. When we extinguish a fire, we put it out. It's out now, and we feel the cold, as we often do when we go outdoors. And when we blow, we *blow out* the candle or the match.
Separable two-word verb *Be careful.*

blow over

Naomi and her family had a terrible fight about her new fiancé, but it's all blown over now. He has been accepted.

After the storm, the winds still may blow a little, but the storm has gone. It has *blown over*. It has gone away from over our heads. It also has the same idea as be over. The storm has finished, it's over.

By extension, we use this for any disturbance.
Two-word verb without an object. *No problem.*

blow up

This is an explosive verb. When you blow something up, it has a tendency to fly up in the air. If terrorists put a big bomb in the road, the explosion can make the victim's car fly a long way. If you blow up a bridge, bits of it will come down minutes later.
Separable two-word verb *Be careful.*

boil
(boil, boiled, boiled)
When you boil water, it turns to steam.

boil down to

When you boil a mixture, a lot of the water escapes as steam. So what is left is concentrated. Lots and lots of people speak in the same way.

The Ex-Minister for Public Affairs spoke for five hours about his obligation to the people who elected him, his duty to the country, and to the need to follow his conscience. What it boiled down to was that he was innocent.

This <u>down</u> has the sense of reduction.

<u>Three-word verb</u> *No problem.*

bottle

(bottle, bottled, bottled)

A glass container that can contain water, wine or Coca-cola. To bottle something means to put it in a bottle. If you bottle your crop of peaches this year, you put them in bottles for the winter.

bottle out

Bottles often have beer. Beer often means courage. <u>Out</u> means away from here or not in the story any more. So if someone *bottles out*, it means they have lost their courage.

Damon thought that the blond in the corner was stunning, and he wanted to talk to her more than anything else in the world. But he bottled out. He never said a word, so he went home alone and sad.

<u>Two-word verb without an object</u> *No problem.*

break
(break, broke, broken)

The basic meaning of *break* is to destroy something rigid. You break a branch or a piece of chocolate by bending it until it snaps into two pieces. You break a fridge by dropping it five floors.

break away

Away means separate.

Imagine a large flock of birds flying south for the winter. A small group may suddenly change direction. It will *break away* from the flock.

In several countries, there are smaller regions that have their own distinctive culture. Sometimes they want to *break away* from the main country. Split away means almost exactly the same.

Two-word verb without an object. No problem.

break down

The beer is warm, Isabel, because the fridge has broken down.

Something big and mechanical, when it breaks, often just sits there and doesn't move. A car, for instance, is down on the road, useless. It's *broken down*. You must call for the break-down truck to come and take it away.

By extension;

Talks between the political parties of the

province have broken down. They are not speaking to each other now.

We also use this phrase for a human when their minds break under the strain of living. We say that they are having a nervous breakdown.
<u>Two-word verb without an object</u>. No problem.

break it down

'Sales are €123,456,789 for the year. Could you break it down into departments? What did each department sell?'
To *break* something <u>down</u> means *'to break something into components'*. Usually an idea, or a number.
Andrea says that she hates maths at school. It's always too complicated and the teacher doesn't break it down into simple pieces.
<u>Separable two-word verb</u>   Be careful.

break in, break into, break out, break out of

A burglar - a kind of thief who enters (goes <u>in</u>) buildings by breaking windows or doors - 'earns' his living by *breaking in*. He breaks into people's houses and steals what he can find. In English law this is known as 'breaking and entering'.
If he is unlucky, he will find himself in a prison. A prison is designed to be very difficult to break out of. It is very, very, very

unlikely that he will ever break out.

Alfred, who plays his guitar every night in the street, is trying to break into the music business.

Armando has written a brilliant new screenplay. He expects that this will help him break into Hollywood.

(They feel as if the music business and Hollywood are protected places or castles.)

Poor Paul is bored stiff with his life. He is bored with his job, with his home, and with his friends. He wants to break out of his routine.

(He feels it as a prison, and he wants to *break out of* it.)

Also

Diseases break out when there is a sudden epidemic.

(The disease BREAKS OUT OF its hiding place.) We also say that there has been an *'outbreak'*.

BREAK IN, BREAK OUT Two-word verbs without an object. *No problem.*
BREAK INTO *is an* Inseparable two-word verb *No problem.*
BREAK OUT OF *is a* three-word verb *No problem either.*

break off

Do you like chocolate bars? I do. Could you break a piece off for me? Why don't you break off a piece for your friend? Now we can share it. Thank you.

We often use off to mean separation. For example, cut off.
By extension -

Young Steve was very sad when Sue broke off the engagement. He thought that he was going to marry her. But she changed her mind.
<u>Separable two-word verb</u> Be careful.

break out in

Imagine your body has an infection or some other kind of illness inside. Sooner or later it could break <u>out</u> of your body <u>in</u> unlovely spots or boils. You have broken out in boils. We also say of the same horror, '*Henry has just <u>come out in</u> horrible boils.*'

Compare this to when a disease can break out.
<u>Three-word verb</u> No problem.

break through

President de Gaulle said, 'Every great man became great by breaking through his limitations.'

Break through an imagined barrier to freedom. We break <u>through</u> our fears or our laziness. Every important scientific discovery is called a *break-through*.
<u>Inseparable two-word verb</u> No problem.

break up

Many years ago, an old sailing ship was wrecked on these rocks. It broke up into tiny splinters. There was no piece larger than your hand.

In a phrasal verb, <u>up</u> often means

'completely'. First the woodcutter cuts down a tree, and then he cuts it up into logs. *'fill up a glass'* means *'fill it to the top'*. Here, *break up* means *'break completely, into pieces'*.

By extension;

It was an ugly crowd, throwing bottles and stones everywhere, but at last the police broke it up.

(There was no crowd left. It ceased to exist. The people in it went away in different directions.)

'It's a terrible line. I can't hear anything you say. The signal is all broken up.'

What we all say sometimes on the phone.

<u>Separable two-word verb</u> *Be careful.*

break up with

When a loving relationship is finished, it is over. There is nothing left. It has broken up.

Derek and Rowena have broken up, their relationship is no more. Derek has broken up with Rowena, he says. Rowena says the opposite. She broke up with him.

<u>Three-word verb</u> *No problem.*

bring
(bring, brought, brought)

The basic meaning of *bring* is 'take or carry something towards me'. For example, you could be sitting happily watching the TV, feeling very lazy, and you decide that you want a beer from the fridge. So, naturally, you shout at love of your life who is in the kitchen, *'Darling. Bring me a beer.'*

bring about

George's car accident brought about many disturbances in the life of his family.

About has two or three meanings. One of these meanings is *'near here'* in space, or *'almost now'* in time.

To *bring* something *about* means to bring something (new) about (here). It means to create. If you like philosophy, you might say that you *bring* something from the Unknown to here. You *bring it about*, which means *'make something happen'*. Compare this to come about which means *'to happen'*.
In the United States, Martin Luther King brought about great changes in how black and white people saw each other.

Compare this with
After Martin Luther King, great changes in racial politics came about.
Separable two-word verb *Be careful.*

bring down

The direction towards the earth is down. so it can mean a depressing or sad mood.
Steve brings me down.
Steve depresses me. He makes me unhappy.
Separable two-word verb *Be careful.*

bring off

We frequently use off to mean a change of

state or position (like go off, set off, or take off). When you *bring* something *off*, you bring it away. By extension, when you bring off a project, you also leave it. Why do you leave a project? Because you have completed it. Because it is finished.

When you bring off a project, it is a success. Always.

Compare this with carry off and pull off

Also, a project can come off.

They all mean the same.

Mary Poppy usually plays romantic comedies, but everyone thought she brought it off very well as the evil manipulative wife of a psychopathic killer.

Separable two-word verb Be careful.

bring out

The Dead Beasts have just brought out a new show.

Throgmorton University Press has brought out a new anthology of Medieval Finnish poetry.

Soldiers say that being under fire will bring out the best and the worst qualities in a man.

In the Middle Ages, during the plagues, the town undertakers would go around the houses shouting, 'Bring out your dead! Bring out your dead!'

Now things are a little happier, and bring out means publish (books and so on), release (records, music, films and software), or reveal (your character). You bring these

things <u>out</u> into the world.
<u>Separable two-word verb</u> . Be careful.

bring round

ROUND in many verbs means *'approximately here'* or *'here, but not urgently'* For example, *'go to the pub'* is direct, but *'go round to the pub'* is more relaxed.

I'm calling a friend who is coming round to my house this evening. She asks me, 'Shall I *bring round* a nice bottle of wine?' I tell her I have plenty of wine at home.

But there is another way we use this verb.

Poor Herbert is shocked by the violence on the TV and he has fainted. Mary brings him round with a rag dipped in floor cleaner.

He is conscious now. In a sense, he is here now.

Compare this with <u>come round</u>.
<u>Separable two-word verb</u>   Be careful.

bring up

There are two common meanings of BRING UP.

Remember, <u>up</u> often has the meaning of *'complete'* or *'finished'*. <u>Fill up</u> means *'fill until full'* and <u>grow up</u> means *'finish your growing, or become adult'*.

I am grown up, which usually means that my parents brought me up.

Your schools educate you, but your mother and father bring you up.

The other meaning is really easy to imagine. *The sea was very rough, and Ivan brought up his breakfast.*
This means that we saw his breakfast a second time.
If you take the boat from France to England you will see and hear this a lot.
By extension, it is possible to bring up a topic of conversation, an idea, into the discussion. If you can come up with a new idea, this has the same meaning.
<u>Separable two-word verb</u> *Be careful.*

brush
(brush, brushed, brushed)
What we do with a brush to clean something. We brush the floor, we brush our clothes, and we brush our teeth. When we use a brush with paint, we say that we are painting.

brush off
George's wife, Amethyst, used to get very angry when he lost their money playing bingo, but he just brushed it off. He was back playing the next day.
When you *brush off* a bit of dirt from your clothes, it is a trivial action. It does not talk more than a second or two. Once done, it is forgotten. By extension, to brush off an incident is to dismiss it as trivial, unimportant.
<u>Separable two-word verb</u> *Careful.*

brush up

Quick! Here comes the man or woman of your dreams! You've only got a few seconds! Brush up your hair, your clothes! Adjust your tie if you're wearing one. Get more presentable!

This up is a higher standard than before. Compare this with do up, make up (your face).

Similarly, if we are going to France in the next few days, we might want to *brush up* our French. We get out the old phrase-books and we listen to a few tracks.

<u>Separable two-word verb</u> Careful.

burn
(burn, burned/burnt, burned/burnt)
What fires do.

burn down
When a building burns completely, it burns down to the ground.
<u>Two-word verb without an object</u>. No problem.

burn out
When a fire is out, it has stopped burning. (The heat has gone out from here.)
One day, the sun will go out
A fire extinguisher tries to put out a fire.
If you don't put your cigarettes out you can start a forest fire.
So, when something has burnt out, it has

stopped burning because there is no fuel left, there is nothing left to burn.

A burnt-out rocket falls back to earth, usually.

By extension, a dynamic man or woman who, after years of hard work, starts to lose their ambition, is said to be *burnt out*.
Two-word verb without an object. No problem.

burn up

Verb + up often has the sense of 'completely'. So to burn up means to burn completely.

Confusingly, if it is a building, *burn up* means exactly the same as burn down.
Two-word verb without an object. No problem.

call
(call, called, called)

To call somebody is to phone them or to shout at them from a distance (not necesarily angrily)

To call to somebody *only* means shouting from a distance.

To call somebody a name is exactly the same as naming him.

call after

Usually, after means later in time

Perhaps you were called after one of your grandparents. You have the same name, but they had it first.

Name after has exactly the same meaning.
Separable two-word verb, usually passive, no problem.

call by

I am talking to Maureen on the phone, and she says, *'No problem. I'll call by in a few minutes and give you the plans.'* Good. I can relax. She'll be here soon.

In space, <u>by</u> has the general idea of *'next to'* or *'close to'*. To call by means to come *by* your house or your office. To visit you.

<u>come by</u>, <u>drop by</u>, <u>call round</u>, <u>come round</u>, and <u>drop round</u> all mean the same.

<u>Two-word verb without an object</u> No problem.

call for

You call <u>for</u> a reason. You call for something you want, you demand it. When I go to a shop to buy green pens, the shop owner says he doesn't have any. Why not? Because there is no call for them. There is no demand.

If you say something a little rude, and you offend someone, they may say, *'There's no call for that.'* or *'That was not called for.'* which means that your contribution to the conversation was not not appreciated.

<u>Inseparable two-word verb</u> No problem.

call off

We often use <u>off</u> to mean being away from the intention, as in

Tonight's show <u>is off</u>.

(It has been postponed or cancelled.)

The theatre-owner and the director agreed to call the show off.

(They postponed or cancelled it.)
If your aggressive dog starts to bite your friend, you *call it off*. That is, you order the animal to stop attacking.
Separable two-word verb   Be careful.

call out

The leading candidate was very happy. His supporters were calling out his name for fifteen minutes.

When we call out in the world, we call out loud. We make a lot of noise.
Compare this with speak out.
Separable two-word verb   Be careful.

call somebody out

When you call your friend out on something, you are calling out to the world on to what he or she said. You are challenging your friend to back up his words. You want evidence.
Separable two-word verb   Be careful.

call round

My daughter is very nervous and hasn't eaten anything all day, because her new boyfriend is calling round to our house this evening to introduce himself.

ROUND in many verbs means *'approximately here'* or *'here, but not urgently'* Other expressions like come round, drop round, call by, come by and drop by have the same meaning.
Two-word verb without an object   No problem.

call to
If you call to Vladimir across the street, you are just shouting a friendly hello.
Notice that on the phone we say this differently. We call Matilda on the phone.
Inseparable two-word verb No problem.

call up
In the old days, <u>up</u> was the direction of authority. When you were *called up*, you were called to defend the King against his enemies. You joined the army. You had to.
<u>Sign up</u> and <u>join up</u> also mean that you go in the army, but suggest that you are a volunteer.
Two-word verb without an object Usually passive. No problem.

calm
(calm, calmed, calmed)
To relax, to tranquilize, to sedate, and so on. This verb is not often used on its own.

calm down
The image here is the sea. A calm sea does not have high waves, or winds at high speed. The wind drops to a breeze, and the waves settle into a low swell. The sea is calm.
With an emotional person, who maybe is too excited for his own good, it is often the time for his friends to tell him to *calm down*.

It is also possible, if you are the right kind of person, to *calm somebody down*.
When it takes an object, it is a <u>separable two-word verb</u>
Be careful.

carry
(carry, carried, carried)

The basic idea of *carry* is to transport or to take something from one place to another. Usually we carry something that has some weight. For example, we could <u>take</u> a pen from one room to another, but we would *carry* a sack of wood that weighed some kilos.

Sometimes, what we are carrying is not so much heavy as important.

Happy mothers carry babies.
Criminals can carry guns or illegal drugs.
The biggest ships in the navy are aircraft-carriers.
A building worker may carry a lot of bricks
The groom carries his bride into their new home for the first time.

(I know she doesn't weigh much, but the symbolism does.)

By extension,

Henry earns a good salary in his new job, but he has to carry a lot of responsibility.
Lion-taming is a job that carries some risks.

get carried away

Mary started cooking a little dinner for

four people, but she got carried away, so we had to invite the family next door to help us eat it all.

Get, you may remember, often has the sense of *become*, or for something to happen to you. For example - *get happy, get strong*, or *to get married*. To *get carried away* means that something or someone carried you away.

In the literal sense, of course, it would mean *'kidnapped'* or *'blown by the wind'*, but we never use it like this. We use it to mean *'overcome by enthusiasm to the point where we lose our judgement'*. The original idea, centuries ago, was that it was the soul that was carried away.

Never send Steve to do the shopping. He always gets carried away, and comes home with lots of things we don't need.

Fixed expression. No problem.

carry off

Off frequently means a movement away (like go off on a journey, set off, take off). When you *carry off* something like a project, you take it away. Why do you take it away? Because you have completed it. It is finished. There is nothing more to do. It is perfect..

When you *carry off* a project or a performance, it is a success. Always.

Lilly Luvvey is a comedian, not a Shakespearian actress, but the reviewers all thought she carried it off very well as

Lady McBeth.
Compare this with bring off and pull off.
And also, ladies and gentlemen, this project will come off.
It will be a success.
They all mean the same.
<u>Separable two-word verb</u> *Be careful.*

carry on, carry on with

Sergeant Higgins comes into the room and all the men stop everything in order to salute him. 'Carry on!' he says. And the men continue with their work.

Here, on means 'continue' (go on, for example). You *carry* a project, you take responsibility for it. So carry on means to continue the work.

The difference between carry on and go on is that carry on is an invitation to keep working, while go on is an invitation to keep talking, or moving.
<u>Two-word verb without an object</u>. *No problem.*

You *carry on with* what you were doing before the interruption
For example
'Right, men,' said Sergeant Higgins. 'Carry on with your work.'
<u>Three-word verb</u> *No problem.*

carry out

Marconi said. 'Any fool can have a good idea, and many fools do, but the art lies in

carrying it out.'
This is the idea of developing something, of producing something <u>out</u> in the real world, out there. To carry out a project means to finish it. It means that you have something to show.
<u>Separable two-word verb</u> *Be careful.*

catch
(catch, caught, caught)

The basic idea of *catch* is to take, or to capture, something that is moving. You can catch a ball flying through the air. (but <u>not</u> a ball that is lying on the ground)
We were late, so we had to catch the afternoon train instead of the morning one.
Also, if we are unlucky we can catch a cold or flu or even something worse. Sometimes, when we want to be rude about someone who is perhaps not very quick, we say, *'He's too slow to catch a cold.'*

catch on, catch on to

Mrs Ballantyne's teenage son used to smoke a lot, until one day when he was swimming, he caught on to the fact that this was not a good idea.

Ideas can move fast. In order to understand a new idea you have to *catch on to* it. This means that you have to catch it and <u>hold on</u> to it.

Often we reverse this, and it is the idea that catches on. When an idea - specially a fashion - catches on, it becomes fashionable and acceptable.

When Matilda looked at the Paris fashions that year, she said, 'Miniskirts and football boots! No, it'll never catch on.'

CATCH ON is a <u>two-word verb without an object</u> No problem.
CATCH ON TO is a <u>three-word verb</u> No problem either.

catch out

When the batsman in cricket or baseball hits the ball and a fielder catches the ball before it touches the ground, then the batsman is <u>out</u> of the game. He has been *caught out*.

So if Orlanda is telling us a story about what she did yesterday, and we notice that a detail is not right, then we know that she is lying. She has been caught out. We caught her out in a lie.

<u>Separable two-word verb</u> Be careful.

catch up, catch up with

Carl Lewis was a great sprinter. No other runner could catch up with him.
He was so fast, that nobody else could ever catch him up.

(These are two ways of saying exactly the same thing.)

Remember, <u>up</u> often has the sense of finishing something. If a shoplifter - a thief who steals from shops - runs away, perhaps the store detective will run after him. Maybe he or she is a good runner and catches up with the thief. So he has the thief in his hands.

Poor countries in our world are having big problems in catching up.

Notice that *catch up* and *catch up with* always imply a race. A trapper - a hunter who sets traps - or the police *catch* their prey.

CATCH UP is a <u>separable two-word verb</u> *but frequently does not have an object..*
CATCH UP WITH is a <u>three-word verb</u> *No problem.*

chat
(chat, chatted, chatted)
To talk informally.

chat up
Mario sees a beautiful stranger, Maria, so he goes over to have a happy chat and to make her feel <u>up</u> and happier. What is he doing? He is chatting her up. He hopes the evening will start to get even better.
<u>Separable two-word verb</u> *Be careful.*

check
(check, checked, checked)
To check something means to verify it, to see that it is acceptable.

check in, check out
<u>In</u> usually means what the dictionary says. That means you can 'be in' a room and not

move. You can also 'go in' the bathroom.
You check in to a hotel or to an airport. Later, when you leave the hotel, you check out. You check out of the hotel. Each time, of course, documents are checked or examined.

Check your baggage *in* / *check* your baggage *out*
If you travel with baggage, you *check in* - as above - and you also *check* your baggage *in*.
When it has an object, it is a separable two-word verb Careful.

check up on
Mrs Murgatroyd was not happy about the young man that her daughter had brought home. She had a professional to check up on him, and found that her suspicions were well-founded.
Up, as usual, means *'complete'*. To *check up on* somebody is what a detective does when he wants background information about a person - where he comes from, how much money he has, how many crimes he has committed, and so on.
Three-word verb No problem.

cheer
(cheer, cheered, cheered)
Both a good feeling, and a shout to express that good feeling. To cheer means to shout very loud because you are happy. Just think of the noise when there is a goal in football.

cheer up
If you have been feeling down, a happy friend might walk by and say, *'Cheer up! You're not dead yet.'* This up means a good feeling, of course This friend is trying to cheer you up..
Separable two-word verb   Be careful.

close
(close, closed, closed)
When you close a door, you can't go through it. And when a shop or a factory is closed, you can't buy things there or work there.

close down
When a business closes down, it means that it is not going to open again.
'Business is bad,' said Mr Shopp. *'I have been working hard and losing money for three years. Time to close it down.'*
This down has the sense of 'back to zero'.
Separable two-word verb   Be careful.

come
(come, came, come)
Come is movement towards the speaker. *'Come here!'* means *'Move towards me.'* Sometimes, on the phone (maybe because we are so polite), we imagine things from the listener's position. We say, *'I'll come to your house in an hour.'*

come about

After her ex-husband won the lottery, great changes came about in Delia's life.

One of the meanings of 'about' is 'near here' in space, or 'almost now' in time.

To come about means something (new) comes about (here). It means to be created. If you like philosophy, you might say that something comes from the Unknown to here. It comes about. It happens.

So come about means *'to happen'*. Compare this to bring about which means *'make something happen'*.

'The cat is in the fridge! How did that come about? Did you have anything to do with it?'

Two-word verb without an object. No problem.

come across

Although I didn't understand a word she was saying, our new Chinese teacher came across as a really nice lady.

Come across means that some information, a new idea perhaps, has come across an imaginary table. 'Something comes across' means that 'something is successfully communicated.'

We often use it for an impression, or an image.

Albert was on trial, and he was in big trouble. His main witness was coming across as a compulsive liar.

81

Compare this with get across, get over, put across, and put over.
Two-word verb without an object. No problem.

come across it

I was fed up last night, but then I came across a €100 note that was blowing about in the street. I felt much better after that.

When you *come across* something, it is lying in your path. It is perhaps in your way. You encounter it. You discover it by chance, by accident.
Inseparable two-word verb No problem.

come across with

I had to ask my father seven times, but finally he came across with the money.

The image here is different from come across. You should think of *coming* here *across* a river full of crocodiles *with* an important package.
Three-word verb No problem.

come after

John went after Jane for months, and finally she said yes.

after means later in time.

First, the escaped prisoner was in the wood, and then the dogs were there. The dogs were there *after* the prisoner was.

To go after something means to pursue it, to hunt it, to chase it.

Come after has the same idea, but towards

me, the speaker.
Jane said, 'John came after me for months, so finally I had to say yes.'
<u>Inseparable two-word verb</u> No problem.

come apart

William was a child who was interested in everything, including his father's watch. 'It came apart in my hand, Dad. Sorry.'
Dad's watch is now in pieces.
We use <u>fall apart</u> similarly, but for much bigger things like buildings, or empires.
<u>Two-word verb without an object</u>. No problem.

come at

When the swordsman came at him, Harrison Ford had no choice. He had to shoot.
<u>At</u> has the general sense of being 'the same place, the same time'.
It is often more aggressive than <u>to</u>. So if somebody comes at me, he comes right into my face. It sounds hostile, and it is. It means to physically attack somebody.
The dogs of the house came at him, so Benny the Burglar had to climb a tree and wait to be rescued by police in the morning.
<u>Inseparable two-word verb</u> No problem.

come between

Between usually means a point in the middle of two things. (Many teachers and books will tell you that that is the only

meaning, and that you should use 'among' for three or more things. But if you listen and read carefully you will find that many people break this rule.)
Between the devil and the deep blue sea.
(Old saying that means 'between two horrible choices')
Jack can't read. He wants to go to university. It's a long way between here and there.
So *come between* is simple.
Nothing comes between me and my family. Not my work, not my hobbies, not the taxman. Nothing.
<u>Inseparable two-word verb</u> No problem.

come by

I am talking to Hilda on the phone, and she says, 'No problem. I'll come by tomorrow and give you your Christmas present.' Good. That's another problem solved.
In space, <u>by</u> has the general idea of *'next to'* or *'close to'*. To come by means to come by (your house or your office).
<u>call round</u>, <u>come round</u>, <u>drop round</u>, <u>call by</u>, and <u>drop by</u> all have the same meaning.
<u>Two-word verb without an object</u> No problem.

come by something

Dave was being interviewed by the police. 'So, tell us again. How exactly did you come by this ring?'
When we come by something, it means that

we discover it. And, by extension, we take it.
Inseparable two-word verb No problem.

come down to

Down is real, here and now. (And up is frequently the world of fantasy and imagination.)

When we *come down to* to something, usually it means to get to the heart of the matter, leaving our fantasies behind.

Mrs Solaris. I'm sorry to tell you, but when we come down to it, your son is really lazy.

We could also say -

When we get down to it, your son is really lazy.

The meaning is the same.
Three-word verb No problem.

come down with

Literally, if we are on the ground floor, somebody who lives on the fifth floor will come down to see us.

The direction towards the earth is down. By extension, it can mean a depressing or sad mood.

A *come-down* is when we have been happy, euphoric, or in a high position and then our mood or situation changes for the worse.

I thought I had won the lottery but I had made a mistake with the coupon. What a come-down!

Mr Henderson used to be a university teacher, but now he sweeps the streets.

What a come-down!

Miriam couldn't go to school today. She has come down with a bad cold.
When we are healthy we are usually happy. When we have an illness we are not. We *come down with* measles, for example.
go down with means the same.
<u>Three-word verb</u> No problem.

come forward
The direction in which we are going is <u>forward</u>.
Sometimes there can great trouble in a country, and a new leader will emerge. He will *come forward* from the mass of the people to the podium.
Forward sometimes has a rather formal sense. Think of <u>put forward</u> a suggestion.
<u>Two-word verb without an object</u> No problem.

come in for
When 'Mary's Merry Misadventures' opened in London, it came in for a lot of bad reviews. The play closed in a week.
To *come in* is to arrive. In the old days London or Paris were the places to be. When a new play came in to town, fashionable people were always ready to be critical. If the play was considered below standard, it would *come in for* a lot of criticism. People would be rude about it.
It always has a negative sense, a sense of

unpleasantness.
Whenever Hamish got bad marks at school, he would come in for a lot of shouting at home.
Three-word verb No problem.

come into

George came into nearly a million dollars when his father's uncle died.
If you suddenly have a lot of money you are in a very new experience. You *come into* a lot of money. We only use this, however, for an inheritance, never a lottery.
Fixed expression. No problem.

come off

Off frequently means a change of state or position (like push off or get off). When you *come off* something, you leave it. By extension, when you come off a project, you also leave it. Why do you leave a project? Because it is finished.
When a project comes off, it is a success. Always.
Compare this with the star who can bring off the show. Or the con-man (a clever criminal) who could carry off 'selling' the Eiffel Tower. I believe he sold it several times.
These all mean the same.
Mary Poppy's performance as Lady McBeth came off very well.
She brought it off very well.

87

She carried it off very well.
<u>Two-word verb without an object</u> *No problem.*

come on

This is a simple expression, often used with impatience. It means come to me, or *come* with me *on* the way. There are other ways of saying this.
Let's go!
Hurry up! We don't have all day!
Get moving!
Fixed idiomatic expression.

come out

For many, many years being gay was a heavily-guarded secret. Now, in most countries, it is no longer illegal, but it is still often a cause for shame. When a homosexual publicly declares what he is, we say that he or she has come out (of the closet - a secret hiding-place). She or he has come <u>out</u> in the open.
<u>Two-word verb without an object</u> *No problem.*

come out in

Imagine your body has an infection or some other kind of illness inside. Sooner or later it could come <u>out</u> of your body *in* unlovely scabs or boils. You have *come out in* boils. We can also say, *'The King has just <u>broken out in</u> horrible boils.'*
<u>Three-word verb</u> *No problem.*

come out with

'Kathleen is quite mad, you know. You should hear some of the things she comes out with.'

A great genius was once asked how he had so many ideas. He said that he had only come up with one idea in his lifetime. But once the idea is expressed, it is out in the open for everyone to see.

One day an angry teacher wanted to know who had painted the door handles with sticky paint. He shouted, 'Who did it? Come out with it!'

To *come out with* something usually means to confess it, or to give some other information unexpectedly.

Three-word verb No problem.

come round

The boss has just phoned me. He was very nice and he asked me to come round to his office. Now I'm worried. He was too friendly.

Round in many verbs means *'approximately here'* or *'here, but not urgently'* For example, *'come to my place'* is direct, but *'come round to my place'* is more relaxed.

call round, drop round, call by, come by and drop by all have the same meaning.

But there is another way we use this verb.

Jill fainted at her daughter's wedding, but a few minutes later she came round.

She is conscious now. In a sense, she is here now.
'Jill's come round.'
'Jill's come to'
These mean the same.
Compare this with bring round somebody with a smell of ammonia.
Two-word verb without an object No problem.

come to, come round to

Poor Henrietta is shocked by the violence on the TV and she has fainted. Alice puts a rag dipped in floor cleaner under her nose. She comes to. She is conscious now. She has come to her senses.

We also say come round to mean the same thing.

Another way we use this verb means 'to arrive at'

Mr Salesman was very happy. "I see you have come to the right decision," he said.

If you want to suggest that this took a long time, you might want to say *'come round to the right decision.'*

COME TO as in 'regaining consciousness' is a two-word verb without an object
COME TO with an object is an inseparable two-word verb No problem either.
COME ROUND TO is a three-word verb No problem.

come under

When we classify things we tend to put them under different headings. Normally at the top of the blackboard or the planning sheet we put the most general things down to the most particular ones at the bottom.

At school, physics, chemistry and biology come under the heading of the sciences, while English, French and literature come under the arts.

We can say <u>fall under</u> to say the same thing.
<u>Inseparable two-word verb</u> No problem.

come up against

Often, <u>up</u> has the idea of reaching a limit, while <u>against</u> always has the idea of *'confrontation'*

Esmeralda wanted to be a policewoman, but she came up against the fact that she was not tall enough. So she had to <u>give up</u> her dream.

Come up against a barrier, a strong obstacle to what you want.
<u>Three-word verb</u> No problem.

come up to

Cows usually come up to the electric fence to graze, to eat their grass, even if there is a huge field to choose from.

<u>Up</u> often means reaching a limit.

Come up to means reaching the limit but not crossing it. There is not the sense of frustration that there is with <u>come up against</u>.

The plans for the new motorway lowered the prices of all the houses in the neighbourhood. There were protests

everywhere. Nobody wanted to live next to the noise and the smell. 'But,' said my father. 'If it comes up to it, we'll sell the house anyway. We're not going to live next to that.'
<u>Three-word verb</u> No problem.

come up with

Einstein was once asked how he had so many ideas. He said that he had only *come up with* one idea in his lifetime.

Sometimes in the old days we must have imagined that our minds lived in our stomachs. (Remember bring up in the sense of vomit.) Well, you can certainly <u>bring up</u> a new idea into the conversation.

Also, you can come up with a new idea. It means exactly the same.
<u>Three-word verb</u> No problem.

count
(count, counted, counted)
When you count, you say 1, 2, 3 ....

count down
When you count <u>down</u>, you count backwards, 5, 4, 3, 2, 1, 0.
<u>Two-word verb without an object</u> No problem.

count in, count somebody in

Imagine that I am talking to a few people,

and I suggest that we have a big barbecue next weekend. 'Hey,' says Larry. 'Count me in.' He wants to be included. He is one of the people that you are counting to be <u>in</u> the group.
<u>Separable two-word verb</u> *Be careful.*

count on

Sometimes <u>on</u> has the solid feeling of being on the ground. Edinburgh Castle has stood on that rock a thousand years.

'Hey, Dan. I got a big, bad problem.'
'You can count on me.'
I am solid. I will support you. You can trust me. You can rely on me.
<u>Inseparable two-word verb</u> *No problem*

cross
(cross, crossed, crossed)

To cross something means to go from one side to another. You can cross the road, cross a bridge, or even cross the English Channel.

cross out

When we draw a line through a word on paper, we are crossing the word <u>out</u> of our minds. Maybe a teacher has decided that a word is wrong, or maybe there is a list of names in front of a manager.

Who will get the job? Oh, no! Who put that fool on the list? I'll cross him out.
<u>Separable two-word verb</u> Be careful.

cut
(cut, cut, cut)
What you do with a knife, scissors, or a sabre.

cut back, cut back on
Weeds are plants you don't want in your garden. But, of course, they grow there with enthusiasm. So you have to regularly *cut* them *back* to their original state, <u>back</u> from the garden.

Our expenses are like weeds. They are always growing. And, like the gardener, we regularly have to *cut back*. We have to *cut back on* expenses.

CUT BACK usually is a <u>two-word verb without an object</u>, so no problem.
CUT BACK ON is a <u>three-word verb</u> No problem either.

cut down, cut down on
'I've got to cut down on my smoking. I smoke about 100 a day. For my New Years Resolution I'll cut down to only 60 a day. What do you think?'
The direction towards the earth is <u>down</u>.
Brenda cut down on on her fried breakfasts, and cakes, and chocolate. And soon she was going shopping for new clothes with a happy smile on her face.

To *cut down* a number is to dramatically reduce it. After all, cutting down a tree dramatically reduces it to a stump.
CUT DOWN is a <u>two-word verb without an object</u>. No problem.
CUT DOWN ON is a <u>three-word verb</u>. No problem either.

cut in

Like <u>cut off</u> this is a sudden interruption. Sometimes in traffic, when you are just about to move, some maniac pushes his car rudely in front of you. If he is a real maniac, this can sometimes be dangerous. He comes <u>in</u> from the outside, he just cut in.
<u>Two-word verb without an object</u>. No problem

cut off

Sometimes in the winter, mountain villages are cut off. They need emergency support by helicopter.
We can use <u>off</u> to mean disconnected. If your electricity, your phone, your water, or, even worse, your Internet connection is cut off, you are cold, silent, dry, and in the dark.
If a person is cut off, it means that they do not inherit anything from the family.
Morty was a gambler, waiting for the day his wealthy father would die. But he lost the bet. His father cut him off without a penny..
<u>Separable two-word verb</u> Be careful.

cut out

Billy Blubber, a fat man who is getting

fatter every day, should not have got that job in the chocolate factory. He is definitely not cut out for the job.

A tailor cuts a suit <u>out</u> from a piece of cloth. And then, we hope, the suit fits perfectly. By extension, if somebody feels that he is not suitable for a certain kind of work, he may say that he is not cut out for it.

Mary, a quiet studious girl, was not cut out to be a bingo caller.
Always passive.

cut up

If you are cut, it is painful and damaging. <u>Up</u> here means completely, so to cut something up is to cut it into little pieces.

'Where is George?'
'Didn't you hear? He lost his job, and disappeared.'
'Why? I thought he was good at it.'
'He was cut up about his wife running away.'

When we say someone is cut up about something, it means that they are destroyed.
Always passive.

deal
(deal, dealt, dealt)

One of the commonest meanings of deal is at the card table. The dealer is the one who distributes the cards.

deal in, deal out

So you can deal someone in, which means to include them, or the opposite, deal them out, to exclude them.
We often extend this to deal out an idea or a project.
'What do think of going to Bournemouth this weekend?'
'I wouldn't deal it out.'
(I wouldn't reject it.)
<u>Separable two-word verb</u> Be careful.

deal with

'How does Amaryllis deal with having three children and no husband?'
'A lot of hard work and plenty of patience.'
Which means 'How does Amaryllis do what is necessary with the cards she has been dealt?'
<u>Inseparable two-word verb</u> No problem.

die

(die, died, died)
The last thing we all do.

die away

Like <u>die down</u>, this refers to sound, but *die away* means music or noise slowly disappearing to silence. Sometimes in music the effect is of the music going far, far away - never to return. It can be sad. It can be

beautiful.
Two-word verb without an object No problem.

die down

We say that a noisy audience in the cinema is very 'lively'. But, gradually, if the film is any good, the noise dies down. It subsides to only a few whispers and sweets being unwrapped.
Two-word verb without an object No problem.

die off

Die is individual. Die off is collective, usually in huge numbers whose individuals don't interest us, such as insects or plants. When there is an ecological catastrophe, such as an oil spill or a forest fire, we always speak of animals *dying off* in large quantities.

It is not as bad as die out. It does not mean the extinction of a species.
Two-word verb without an object No problem.

die out

To die is individual. To die out is collective. It is the end of a species. There are no more of them out in the world. This is the end.

250 million years ago, 95% of the species on Earth died out.
Two-word verb without an object No problem.

do

(do, did, done)

DO is the most general action verb in the language. It has the basic meaning of *'action'* or *'work'* (in distinction to make, which has the basic meaning of *'create something new'*)

It is the only verb in the language that can stand for another verb (in the same way as a pronoun stands for a noun that we mentioned before).

For example,
'I like Mr Dullman.'
'I don't.'

It is also an auxiliary verb. We use it for making questions, and for forming negatives with all verbs except other auxiliary verbs.
'Do you smoke?'
'No, I don't.'

We also use it occasionally for emphasising a positive sentence.

In these cases, the *'do'* is *always* emphasised. *'I do like her.'*

do away with

Away means you never see them again

To do away with somebody is an old sinister expression meaning to kill them and dispose of (*do away with*) the body.
Three-word verb. No problem.

do in

To do somebody in is a cheerful old

expression meaning to kill them. You will find it in books by Dickens and in Sherlock Holmes stories.
Separable two-word verb Careful.

do up

This is up to a higher standard than before. (Like make up)
When you do up your house or a flat, you renovate it. You are doing work on it, to take it up to a higher standard. You can also fix up your house.
Separable two-word verb Careful.
Do up your jacket, your suitcase, or your shoes. This means to fasten them.
Separable two-word verb Careful.

do with

Usually a fixed expression. I could do with that, meaning I could use that.
'Did you hear about that man down the road who won the lottery?'
'How much did he get?'
'About ten million, they say.'
'I could do with that.'
Inseparable two-word verb No problem.

do without

What do poor people do? They *do without* lots of the good things in life. They do without.
'Mum! I want a motorbike, and I haven't got the money!'

'Hard luck, son! You'll just have to do without.'
go without means exactly the same.
<u>Inseparable two-word verb</u>, *usually without an object. No problem.*

dress
(dress, dressed, dressed)

To dress means to put your clothes on. The room that actors use before they go on stage is the dressing room.

dress up

<u>Up</u> as so often means to a higher standard. So you dress up when you go to a wedding. You put on your best clothes. There was a song of many years ago called All Dressed Up and Nowhere to Go.
<u>Inseparable two-word verb</u>, *without an object. No problem.*

drink
(drink, drank, drunk)

What we do to beer, tea, Coca-cola, and so on.

drink up

'Time, ladies and gentlemen, please! Drink up now! Haven't you got homes to go to?'
You will hear this at closing time in a British pub.
Here, <u>up</u> means to finish. So *drink up* means to finish your drink.

Separable two-word verb but usually without an object. Careful.

drop
(drop, dropped, dropped)
To drop something is to allow it to fall.

drop back
This means exactly the same as <u>fall back</u>. If you are in front in a race, but then someone else flies past you, then you have dropped <u>back</u>, you have fallen back.
<u>Two-word verb without an object</u> No problem.

drop by
I was talking to Mrs Kitchener on the phone, and she said, 'No problem. I'll drop by in a few minutes and give you the potatoes.'
In space, <u>by</u> has the general idea of 'next to' or 'close to'. To DROP BY means to drop (from Heaven?) by (your house or your office)
<u>call by</u>, <u>come by</u>, <u>call round</u>, <u>come round</u>, and <u>drop round</u> all have the same meaning.
<u>Two-word verb without an object</u> No problem.

drop in, drop in on
Mora lives up the street. She's always dropping in for a cup of tea.
When angels visit you <u>in</u> your home, they drop in from Heaven. You, of course, feel exactly the same way when a friend comes

to visit you.

Now we're here in Ealing, why don't we drop in on Ken? He'd love to see us.

DROP IN is a two-word verb without an object No problem.
DROP IN ON is a three-word verb No problem either.

drop off, drop something off

'Hello, Clive. Is that you? You left your umbrella at my car last night: No problem. I'll drive round to your house later, and drop it off.'

When you *drop off* something, or you *drop something off*, you are delivering it.
Separable two-word verb Be careful.

Drop off also means to drop off from consciousness. In simpler words, to fall asleep, usually rather suddenly.

Mr Monotone, the ecclesiastical history teacher, was talking and talking, and I just dropped off.
Two-word verb without an object No problem.

drop out

The rat-race is how we often describe the rush for a good education, a good job, a nice house in a nice area, a beautiful husband or wife, and everything else we want. People who *drop out* of this race - who allow themselves to fall out of the competition - are people who abandon school early, give up their chances for a good job, and who

generally don't live in a nice house in a nice area.
Two-word verb without an object *No problem.*

drop round

Round usually means *'approximately here'* or *'here, but not urgently'* For example, *'come to my house'* is very direct, but *'come round to my house'* is friendly.
I'm calling a friend who is dropping round this evening. She says, 'Who else is coming?'
call round, come round, call by, come by and drop by all mean the same.
Two-word verb without an object *No problem.*

dry
(dry, dried, dried)
A dry day is a day when it does not rain. A dry cloth has no water in it. So to dry something means to remove the water from it.

dry out

This out means *'away'* so when you dry something out it means that you eliminate all the water in it; the water goes away. Imagine that you have been caught in the rain and your clothes are wet when you get home. You have to dry them out before you can wear them again.
Separable two-word verb *Be careful.*

dry up

Dry completely (which is the most common meaning of up) When a river dries up there is no more water in it. The sun dried it up. When farming land dries up there is tragedy and people have to move away.
Separable two-word verb Be careful.

end, end up
(end, ended, ended)

To end means to finish. Up most often means the same. So to end up means the definite, last, final, end result of something or someone.

'What happened to Mrs Mouse?'
'She ended up in an old people's home, terrorising everyone.'
END UP *Two-word verb without an object No problem.*

face
(face, faced, faced)

Your face is the part in front of your head where most of your personality lives. When you face something you turn your face to it. Sometimes this is an act of courage.

face up to

If you face something that is bigger than you are, you face up to it. This is always brave. In fact, a coward is somebody who never faces up to anything.

It is human nature to respect and admire someone who faces up to a tragedy, for a example.
Three-word verb No problem.

fall
(fall, fell, fallen)
What happens to things when nothing holds them up.

fall about
One of the meanings of about is *'all over the place'*. Why did we fall all over the place? Because we were laughing so hard that we couldn't stand up. Have you ever seen a child - or an adult - fall off a chair from laughing so much?
One of my favourite verbs.
Two-word verb without an object No problem.

fall apart
When something falls apart, it collapses. Its component parts separate. Imagine a bridge in an earthquake.
For smaller things, we say come apart.
Two-word verb without an object No problem.

fall away
Music can fall away to nothing. Just like die away it means that the music gradually disappears. It feels as if it is slowly falling to earth.

Two-word verb without an object No problem.

fall back

This means the same as drop back. When you fall back in a race you are losing.
Two-word verb without an object No problem

fall back on

When things become difficult we sometimes have to fall back on our reserves, like a fat man in a famine. We have to go back to an earlier place.

Oh, dear. The washing machine's broken down. I'm on holiday, so you kids will have to fall back on washing everything by hand.
Three-word verb No problem.

fall behind

This idea is really similar to fall back and drop back but we use it more for the race of life. If a child falls behind at school, his parents are not happy. Some people get ahead and others fall behind. In fact, there used to be a political slogan in the United States about education. No child left behind.
Two-word verb without an object No problem.

fall behind with

Why is Zoe staying so late in the office every night? Because she *fell behind with* her work, and she has to work long hours to catch up.

Three-word verb No problem.

fall down

A badly-constructed building can fall down. By analogy, so can a badly-constructed argument.

Mr Archer's lawsuit against a newspaper for defamation - for printing lies about him - fell down when it was discovered that he had paid bribes to the important witnesses.

Two-word verb without an object No problem.

fall for

An email came for Mr Wally telling him about a fortune in Nigeria. He fell for it and paid several thousand euros to help his new friend bring the money to Europe. Poor Mr Wally!

When we fall for someone we fall in love with them. They are beautiful, kind, funny and intelligent. They are wonderful and everything they do is perfect. Everything they say or think is perfect......

But this is not Paradise or the Garden of Eden. Some people make mistakes, some people tell lies, and some other people believe them.

Inseparable two-word verb No problem.

fall in

I leave this to your imagination. What can someone fall in that is really unpleasant and disagreeable? It smells really bad, too!

'I thought Walter was going fine, but then he fell right in it.'
This means that we can all laugh at Walter.
<u>Inseparable two-word verb</u> *No problem.*

fall in with

Uncle Tom used to be such a nice man, but he fell in with a bad crowd. He started choosing bad people as friends. Notice that it is easier to fall than to rise.
<u>Three-word verb</u> *No problem.*

fall off

We often use <u>off</u> to mean being away from the target, or the hope.
When we look at a graph, we often imagine that the lines have weight, that it is easier to go down than to go up. The sales figures of a company can show this. When a product is becoming less popular, we say that demand has *fallen off*.
<u>Two-word verb without an object</u> *No problem.*

fall on

They fell on him like a pack of wolves.
(A gang of them together attacked him until he was on the ground)
<u>On</u> can be aggressive.
Imagine a ton of sand *fell on* you. You would be buried and helpless. If you are attacked by many people at once, you have the same situation. You can't defend yourself.
They fell on him like a ton of something

smelly.
<u>Inseparable two-word verb</u> No problem.

fall out, fall out with

When you are with your friends, it is a nice feeling like being in a warm room with a fire on a cold day in winter. But friends can sometimes *fall out* (of friendship). They are no longer friends. The bonds that held them together are not there any more. It always implies bad feeling.
<u>Two-word verb without an object</u> No problem.

When two friends fall out, they *fall out with* each other.
'I thought Brenda and Belinda were best friends forever.'
'They were, but Brenda fell out with Belinda over some boy.'
<u>Three-word verb</u>. No problem.

fall over

We walk on the ice. Whoops! We *fall over*. Our head is on the ground and our feet are in the air. We have fallen and we are all over the ice like a fool, and our friends are laughing at us.
Notice that we never use this verb to talk about falling from a higher place to a lower one.
<u>Two-word verb without an object</u> No problem.

fall through

Reggie was going to marry Rowena, but

everything fell through. Reggie became a sailor and Rowena went to a convent.

Imagine that your plans are written on paper and that your plans drop <u>through</u> a hole in the floor. (In Britain, many floors are made of wood so this is not impossible.) Your plans will have fallen through the gap. Your plans will have fallen through.

Any plan that has *fallen through* has failed, or has not even been started.

<u>Two-word verb without an object</u> *No problem.*

fall under

Imagine a teacher drawing a diagram of life on earth. There are animals, plants, and fungi that all fall <u>under</u> the category of life. In the animal category, there are reptiles, insects, mammals and many other things. These all fall under the category of animals. <u>Come under</u> means exactly the same.

<u>Inseparable two-word verb</u> *No problem.*

feel

(feel, felt, felt)

My favourite definition is to have an inward persuasion of something.

feel down

<u>Down</u> here means depressed, not happy, and that is exactly what feeling down means.

<u>Two-word verb without an object</u> *No problem.*

feel up to

Up is happy and strong. Feel up to something is to feel strong enough to do it.
'Do you want to go out with me tonight, Molly?'
'I'm tired, Mikey. I have had a long and horrible day. I don't feel up to it.'
Three-word verb No problem.

figure
(figure, figured, figured)
To figure is an old expression meaning to think deliberately. Like *reckon* it is much more common in the United States than in Britain.

figure out

When you figure out a problem, you have solved it by thinking. Out is often a conclusion. It means the same as to work out a problem or a puzzle.
'When Nora found her husband very very close to her best friend, she finally figured out that he had married her for her money.'
Separable two-word verb Be careful.

fill
(fill, filled, filled)
When you fill a glass, you put, perhaps, beer into it.

fill in, fill out

You want to register, you have to *fill in* a form. You go to the tax office, you must fill in twenty forms. You go to the bank for money, it is necessary to fill in even more forms.

Forms without you are empty and useless. You have to fill them in.

All this is British English. In the United States, you have to *fill out* these forms. A form is a sheet of paper out in front of you. (Think of lay out and set out your goods on a market stall.) You have to *fill* the thing *out*.

<u>Separable two-word verbs</u>. *Be careful.*

fill up

'I have eaten too much Christmas dinner. I can't move. I'm full up.'

Up often means 'complete'. To fill up means to fill something until it is full.

' How much do you want? says the man at the filling station.
'Fill it up, please.'
(He wants a full tank.)

<u>Separable two-word verb</u>   *Careful.*

find
(find, found, found)

When you find something, you now know where it is. You did not know before.

113

find out

When you find something <u>out</u> in the open, you discover it. (Look at the word dis-cover. It is saying the same thing in a different way. Something was *'covered'* or *'hidden'* and now it is in the open.)

Some people say that journalists, psychiatrists, and spies are very similar. They all spend their lives trying to find out the truth about other people.

<u>Separable two-word verb</u> Careful.

fit
(fit, fit, fit)

A door fits the doorway. Your car fits the garage, we hope. How many bottles fit in a case? Usually twelve. Do your feet fit your shoes? If not, you are going to be uncomfortable. Can you fit in to last year's clothes? Time to stop eating for a week.

Fit means to fully occupy a space. How many people can fit into that room?

fit in

Fit in also has a social meaning.

Penelope does not like her new school, because the other kids don't like her. She is not the same as the rest. She doesn't fit in.

<u>Two-word verb without an object</u> No problem.

fix
(fixed, fixed, fixed)

The commonest meaning of fix is to repair

something. Another meaning is to arrange or prepare. Americans fix breakfast, for example.

fix up

Fix up means the same as do up. You fix something up to a higher standard. Sometimes people buy an old house cheap and fix it up to sell for a profit. Such a house is often called a 'fixer-upper'
Separable two-word verb   Be careful.

follow
(follow, followed, followed)

When something moves and you move after it, you are following it. Every leader has followers (by definition). A follower of fashion always keeps up with fashion. She is always in fashion.

follow through

You follow a project through to the end. You complete it. You follow it through. This is similar in meaning to get through something, but notice that the grammar is different. You *follow it through*, but you *get through it*.

Notice a difference in meaning. When we say that Jim followed it through, we mean that he achieved something. Good man, Jim! He didn't stop halfway. He has something to show for it. But if we say he got through it, it merely means that he

survived.
Separable two-word verb   Be careful.

follow up
You ask a company for some information about their latest super product you must have, and they send you a nice catalogue. A few days later, they phone you to 'see if you got the catalogue'. That was a follow-up call. The company was following up. Up here, as so often, means completing.
Separable two-word verb   Be careful.

get
(get, got, got (US gotten))
What does *get* mean?
Well, *get + (noun)* means 'achieve', 'receive', 'obtain' etc.
Get a new car. Get my salary every month. Get a bad headache.

And *get + (adjective / past participle)* means 'become'.
Get rich. Get even fatter. Get married.

But the interesting one for us today is *get + (preposition)* which means something like 'move the body somewhere with some difficulty'.
Get in prison. (Oh, dear)
Get out of prison. (More difficult)
Get on your bike
Get under the table during an earthquake.

get about, get around

After his accident, Edwin had to sit in a wheelchair for several months, but it didn't stop him getting about. You could see him all over the town at different social events.

about has several meanings: one of the most common meanings is 'from here to there to somewhere else'.

For example; It's play time, and 300 children are screaming, playing and running *about* the playground.

Get around has exactly the same meaning.

Two-word verb without an object No problem.

get across

To *get something across* means to get some information, a new idea perhaps, across an imaginary table. *'To get something across'* means *'to successfully communicate it'*.

A wise man at the top of the mountain has his knowledge in a bag. He's handing it to you. But you are perhaps a little slow. So it takes time to get it across. It takes time for the message to *get across..*

It takes time for the message to get over. Same meaning.

Get across is very similar to put across and put over, but there is the slight sense - that you always have with *get* - of a little difficulty.

GET something ACROSS is a separable two-word verb Be careful.

———

117

The message, the information, or the impression *gets across*.

Also, the message can come across. Same meaning.

GET ACROSS *is a* two-word verb without an object *No problem.*

get ahead

In any race, the person, horse or car in front of the others, the one who is winning, is ahead.

Many of us think that life is a race. At the beginning, all the runners are together, but, sooner or later, some of them start *getting ahead*. They are winning, and the cameras are on them.

(The others that we don't notice start to get behind. or fall behind)

All ambitious people - and usually their parents as well - want to get ahead.

Fixed expression.

get along

Jimmie has a problem at work. He doesn't get along with his colleagues at all. Whatever they do, they just don't get along. They can't work together.

When two people *get along* (we often say get on), it means that they are comfortable together. For example, they can work together in the same office without trouble.

By extension, one of the two *gets along with* the other.

GET ALONG *is more American than British English. The*

equivalent is <u>get on</u>.
GET ALONG is a <u>two-word verb without an object</u>   No problem.
GET ALONG WITH is a <u>three-word verb</u>. No problem either.

get at

Why do they have bars in the lions' cages in the zoo? Is it so that the lions can't get at the little boys, or so that the little boys can't get at the lions?

<u>At</u> is frequently more confrontational and aggressive than <u>to</u>. (Think of <u>come at</u>, compared with come to me, which is welcoming.)

To *get at* something means to reach it, to be able to touch it.

<u>Inseparable two-word verb</u> *No problem.*

get away with

<u>Away</u> means you never see it again

When you rob a bank (Remember, you steal the money but you rob the owner), you have to *get away* fast. However, getting away is not much use if you are not carrying large sacks of money. You have to *get away with* the money.

By extension, we talk of somebody *getting away with* a crime, when we mean he commits a crime and escapes punishment.

In Victorian London, there was a famous serial killer called Jack the Ripper. He was never caught. He got away with it. He got away with murder.

<u>Three-word verb</u>. *No problem.*

get back at

Get at means something aggressive, as at can do, and back nearly always has the sense of 'return', so to get back at someone means revenge. You get back at the (insulting word) because he first got at you.
There was a case in England some years ago about a spy working for one of the government listening posts. He betrayed his wife and his country in some way. She 'forgave' him and he confessed to her, but she *got back at* him by giving him up. She got a divorce and he got fourteen years.
Three-word verb *No problem.*

get back into

Apart from the literal meaning, *It was dawn so Dracula got back into his coffin*, this follows from be into.
Doris really likes Spanish Muslim architecture. She was really into it, but she had too many things to do. Years later, when her children could live by themselves, she got back into it.
Three-word verb *No problem.*

get behind

Samantha's parents are very worried. When they read her reports from school, they fear that she is getting behind, so they are hiring a special teacher.
Life is often a race, we think. At the beginning, all the runners are together, but,

sooner or later, some of them start to <u>get ahead</u>. They are winning, and they win the prizes, but the others that we don't notice are *getting behind*.

<u>Falling behind</u> means exactly the same.
Fixed expression.

get by

In space, <u>by</u> has the general idea of 'next to' or 'close to'. When you are in the cinema happily waiting for the film to start, there is always someone late who has to push past your knees. To get by an obstacle means to get past the obstacle with a little difficulty.

By extension, poor people find that getting by the obstacles of life more difficult. So that *getting by* is now the idea of 'surviving a hard life'.

You may well have seen simple English teaching books with titles like 'Get By in English'. The idea is to survive in English.
<u>*Two-word verb without an object*</u> *No problem.*

get down to

Mrs Higgins. I'm sorry to tell you, but when we get down to it, your son is a lazy pudding.

Work is normally a serious down-to-earth activity. It is practical, so when we get <u>down</u> to it, usually it means we *get down to* something serious. Sometimes, by extension, it means to get to the heart of the matter.

We could also say
When we <u>come down to</u> it, your son doesn't like working.
The meaning is the same.
<u>Three-word verb</u>. No problem.

get into

Quite recent, I think. To get into something is to be absorbed by it, to be fascinated by it.
Julian hated the idea of studying the history of statistical methods, but he gradually got into it, and now he <u>is into</u> it and has become an expert.
<u>Inseparable two-word verb</u> No problem.

get off, get off on

Edwina gets off on parties every weekend. She doesn't sleep till Sunday night.
Thousands of airplanes are <u>taking off</u> every hour all round the world.
Get off is a non-literal extension of this idea. Originally, I think, druggie slang from the 60s, it means to get <u>off</u> from their boring everyday lives on the ground, and to 'fly' in the world of drugged fantasy. Now, it means anything that gets you really excited.
Get off on means the stimulus.
Steve gets off on motorbikes. He has already had several accidents, but he won't stop.
By the time you read this, this verb may be very dated. That is to say, very old-fashioned.

GET OFF is a two-word verb without an object No problem.
GET OFF ON is a three-word verb. No problem either.

get off with

<u>Off</u> here is away from this place. To get someone away from this place, a good method is to be charming and desirable. Andy got off with Mandy is a casual way of saying that Andy, with his good looks and his charm, persuaded Mandy to leave this place and go somewhere more comfortable and private.
Three-word verb No problem.

get on

'Ivan! I haven't seen you for years. How are you getting on?'
We frequently use <u>on</u> in the sense of continue - as in <u>carry on</u> - and a common question of two old friends who haven't seen each other for a while is 'How are you getting on?' Another expression we use when we talking about somebody who is not young, is that they are getting on a bit.
'How's your mum?'
'Oh, she's fine. She's getting on a bit. She'll be ninety next June.'

When two people get on (sometimes Americans say <u>get along</u>), it means that they are comfortable together. For example, they can work together in the same office without trouble.

By extension, one of the two gets on with the other.

Jean has no problems at work. She gets on with her boss. They get on fine.
GET ON is a two-word verb without an object. No problem.
GET ON WITH is a three-word verb. No problem

get out
Get out! means get out of here now. This is my house and you are not welcome.
Fixed expression. No problem.

get out of
Get has three main meanings, depending on what follows it. The literal meaning of get out of is to leave something with a little difficulty, perhaps. Miriam didn't like her boyfriend's car. It was hard to get out of.

But the question *What do you get out of it?* is asking what thing do you get? This get means achieve or obtain. So, *What do you get out of being rude to the tax inspector?* means what benefit do you get?
Three-word verb No problem.

get over
To get something over means to get some information, some teaching, some new ideas perhaps, over an imaginary table. 'To get something over' means 'to successfully communicate it'.

A great mathematician is teaching the

quantum mechanics class. This is hard. The ideas are not getting over today.

It takes patience for the message to get across. Same meaning

Get it over is very similar to put over and put across, but there is the slight sense - that you always have with *get* - of a little difficulty.

GET IT OVER is a separable two-word verb   Be careful.

The message, the information, or the impression *gets over*.

Careful. This has a completely different meaning from GET OVER IT.

This GET OVER is a two-word verb without an object No problem.

get over it

Poor George never did get over the death of his wife. He thought about her every hour of every day for the rest of his life.

Imagine, dear reader, that you are standing next to a wall that is two metres high. Normally you would not even think of getting over it, but suddenly there is a large, horrible, angry bull and.he doesn't like you. No problem. *You would get over that wall.*

For English speakers, a bad illness, an emotional loss, an acute disappointment are all walls that you have to get over. This over means 'finished'.

Mary took months to get over her flu.

Notice the difference between GET OVER IT and GET IT OVER.

GET OVER something is an <u>Inseparable two-word verb</u>
No problem.

get it over, get it over with

Here, <u>over</u> means 'finished', 'complete' or 'we don't have to think about it any more'. Like be over and blow over.

Many people don't enjoy visiting the dentist very much. So they schedule the appointment for as early in the day as possible. They want to *get it over with*, get it <u>finished</u>, so they can relax for the rest of the day.

GET IT OVER is a <u>separable two-word verb</u>
GET IT OVER WITH is a <u>three-word verb, but it is separable</u>. Notice where the object goes. CAREFUL

get round

George's little daughter Gina is only five years old, but she can get round her father whenever she wants. Everything she wants, she gets.

You want to go down a forest path, and there is a huge tree standing there. It has been there for several hundred years and it is not going to move for you. So you have to *get <u>round</u>* it, however difficult it may be.

Frequently in this life, your obstacle will be another person (who is as stubborn as a tree and is not going to move for you). So what do you do? You have to *get round* him. You have to persuade him.

<u>Inseparable two-word verb</u> *No problem.*

get round to

It's funny, but Paul never seems to get round to doing the ironing. There is never enough time.

Get always implies at least a little difficulty. (*Go in* a room is simple, *get in* suggests that there was a problem. Maybe you had to enter through the window.) *Go round* the village is simple. The postman does it every day. *Get round* is harder.

If you have a lot of work, maybe it takes time to get round to everything.

One of the hardest things of my life is GETTING ROUND TO answering all my e-mails.

Three-word verb. No problem.

get through

Mr Kowalski spends 12 hours a day at the office. He gets through twice as much work as the rest.

Imagine something. You are in a Hollywood-style jungle. There are leaves and branches everywhere, and you must use a machete to get through the jungle. Hard, isn't it? How would you feel after 100 metres of that? To get through something you must be inside it and trying to get outside at the far side.

If you have a lot of work, don't you feel as if you are inside it?

Fat George gets through ten hamburgers a day.

(It was a lot of work.)

Go through and run through have similar, but not identical meanings.
Today, I *got through* a lot of work. (So I'm tired.)
Today, I went though a lot of work. (So I'm happy.)
Today, I *ran through* a lot of work. (Easy. Do you want me to do more?)
Inseparable two-word verb No problem.

get through, get through to

Through means movement from outside of something, in to it, and then outside it again.

We imagine a cable or a phone line as a pipe. Electricity or information goes through the cable.

In the old days when you phoned somebody at work, you had to go through the switchboard. You had to speak to the nice receptionist and persuade her to connect you to the right person. You wanted to be put through. When that happened she would say, 'Putting you through.'

When this had happened you had *got through*. You had got through to the person you wanted.

Sometimes we use this expression when we talk about talking to slow, stubborn or hysterical people. It can be very difficult to

get through to them.
GET THROUGH is a <u>two-word verb without an object</u> No problem.
GET THROUGH TO is a <u>three-word verb</u>. No problem either.

get up
What do you do most mornings? You get <u>up</u> (out of bed).
<u>Two-word verb without an object</u> *No problem.*

give
(give, gave, given)
Everybody knows what give means. Children probably learn it about the same time as <u>take</u>. You give me a present, I take it.

give away
Sebastian felt bad about being rich, so he gave all his money away.
(He gave it all to charity perhaps.)
<u>Away</u> always has the sense of great distance. *Far away* is further than just *far*. So, to *give* something *away* means to give it so you won't see it again.

WITH PRICES SO CHEAP, WE'RE ALMOST GIVING IT AWAY!!!
(Advertising slogan for a supermarket)
<u>Separable two-word verb</u> *Be careful.*

give in
<u>Give</u> can sometimes have the sense of

'yield'. (give way, for example)
When two boys are pushing each other, half-playing and half-fighting, one will, sooner or later, push into the other so the weaker one will have to yield. The threat is in his space. He will have to surrender. He will have to *give in*.

Two-word verb without an object No problem.

give off

That cheese you brought back from France gave off such a horrible smell that we had to throw out all the food in the fridge. Thanks, Mary.

We say off for the idea *'away from the point'* or *'away from here'*. Some chemicals, like ammonia, *give off* a really interesting intense smell. If you don't believe me, try it for yourself. A burning rubber tyre dump gives off thick black smoke.

Separable two-word verb but we rarely use it with only a pronoun. Usually, the word order is 'GIVE OFF something'. So no problem.

give out

My granny lived till she was 94 years old, but then her heart gave out.

Give can sometimes have a sense of 'yield' as in give in or give up.
Give out has the sense of giving out your last breath. You breathe no more. You are dead.

Sometimes, it is less dramatic,
I used to play football every day, but then my knees gave out.
(So I should never play football again.)
<u>Two-word verb without an object</u>. *No problem.*

give up, give somebody up

Amanda went to see the doctor and he told her to give up smoking immediately. So she stopped that day. She has never smoked since.
The doctor said, 'Give it up! Otherwise it will kill you.'
Heaven is <u>up</u>. When you *give* something *up*, you are giving it to Heaven. You are renouncing it. You don't need it any longer on this earth. It's a sacrifice.
<u>Separable two-word verb</u> *Be careful.*

By extension, *give up* without an object means to surrender.
After being hit dozens of times, Billy the Bad Boxer at last gave up.
He sacrificed his dream. He stopped boxing.
<u>Two-word verb without an object</u>. *No problem.*

But *give somebody up* has a slightly different image, and a totally different meaning. Here, <u>up</u> is the direction of authority, the law or justice. So to give somebody up means to deliver them to justice, to the police.

Years ago in Britain, there was some kind of electronic spy who confessed to his wife what he had done. She wanted a divorce so she *gave him up* to the law. She got her divorce, and he got fourteen years. You could also say that she turned him in.
Separable two-word verb . Be careful.

give way

Give can sometimes have the sense of *'yield'*. If a lady and a gentleman arrive at the same door at the same time, the gentleman - if he is a gentleman - will *give way*. He will give the lady the way through the door. He will yield.

Sometimes in Britain, you will see road signs that say GIVE WAY. This means that you must give the *'right of way'*, you give priority to the cars on the other road.

Rarely, a bridge will collapse. Somewhere in the structure, a metal beam gave way. It was not strong enough.
Two-word verb without an object No problem.

go
(go, went, gone)

Go generally means 'move', often in the direction away from me, but never towards me. It also means 'function'

go after

John went after Jane for months, and finally she said yes.

(Another version)

John went after Jane for months, and she finally caught him.

Usually, after means later in time

To *go after* something means to follow it. First, the escaped prisoner was in the wood, and then the dogs were there. The dogs were there *after* the prisoner was.

Now, to go after something means to pursue it, to hunt it, to chase it.

Steven went after that job for a long time. I don't know if he got it.

Compare this with come after.

Inseparable two-word verb No problem.

go ahead

Ahead is an old word for forward, the direction in which we are going.

I asked my boss about whether I should go to our other factory to look at the problem. He told me to go ahead.

When we say *Go ahead!* we giving permission to go, just like a green traffic light.

Two-word verb without an object. No problem.

go at, have a go at

At has the general idea of two things, same place, same time. *Go at* has two meanings that are similar but not exactly the same.

Go at somebody means to move right up to their faces. It's very aggressive.

That rottweiler is dangerous. It just went

at me.

And *go at something* means to attack a job, for example, very aggressively, with lots of enthusiasm.

Steve know nothing about carpentry at first, but he went at it, and now he has finished all the door frames of his new house.

We also say <u>go for</u> in the same two senses.

<u>Inseparable two-word verb</u> *No problem.*

We also say *have a go at* something or someone. It's softer, less intense, than *go at*.

That chihuahua is very bad-tempered. It just had a go at me.

(It tried to bite me.)

I had a go at learning Chinese, but I decided to give up after a few months.

go away

When something or someone goes away, we don't see it again. With some people and some problems, this is our dearest wish. We just want them to go <u>away</u>. Sometimes we even tell them.

There are other, more intense, expressions for the same desire, but this is a book for the whole family.

<u>Two-word verb without an object</u>. *No problem.*

go back, go back on

<u>Back</u> after most verbs has the sense of 'return'. *Go back* is *'return there'*, *come*

back is *'return here'*, *pay back* is *'return the money'* and so on.
Go back is literal.
After his appointment at the dentist, William went back to the office.

But we only use *go back on* in one way. If somebody goes back on his word, it means that he breaks his word. He breaks his promise. He does not do what he said he would do.
Mr Martinez promised to pay me for my work, but he lied. He went back on his word.
<u>Three-word verb</u>. No problem.

go down (well)
Veronica told her husband that she wanted a divorce. It didn't go down very well. He was not happy.
When we eat, the food goes <u>down</u> to our stomach. If the food is delicious, it goes down well. By extension, anything we consume and enjoy, goes down well.
After some months of delay, the President raised taxes on nearly everything. That went down really badly with everyone.
Fixed expressions. No problem.

go down with
Lola couldn't go to school today. She has gone down with a bad cold.
The direction towards the earth is <u>down</u>. By

extension, it can mean a depressing or sad mood.

When we are healthy we are usually happy. When we have an illness we are not. We *go down with* flu, for example.

come down with means exactly the same.
Three-word verb. No problem.

go for

One of the commonest meanings of for is the reason why you do something.

Helen wasn't sure if the job offer was right for her, but we told her to go for it. She did, and now she's the manager.

'It was a risk,' she said. 'But I went for it.'

To *go for it* means to *'go in the direction of it'*. It can be enthusiastic or it can be aggressive.

'I don't like that dog at all. Last week, it went for me.'

Go at is very similar.
Inseparable two-word verb No problem.

go in for

Go in simply means 'to enter'.

Mr Hendrickson rang the doorbell, and went in.

George habitually goes *'in'* for an activity - an activity so absorbing, so exciting, that when he does it, he feels as if he is in it. And one of the commonest meanings of *for* is a purpose. It is the reason why you do something.

Mr Bevis goes in for stamp collecting. Mary goes in for playing the violin.
These are their passions, their hobbies.
<u>Three-word verb</u>. *No problem.*

go in with

Go in with is business. Your partners are the people you go <u>in</u> a venture or a project with.

A major cause of business failure is problems between partners. This means that you must always be very careful of who you go in with.

Contrast this with <u>go out with</u>, which is romantic.

A <u>three-word verb but it is separable</u>. You GO IN (a business) WITH (somebody).

go off

When cheese moves by itself, it has *gone off*. When bread, or eggs, are green, they have gone off. They <u>are off</u>. Not to eat.

Sometimes <u>off</u> means *'away from the point'*, *'away from what we want'* and other times we use <u>off</u> to mean a change of state or position (like <u>push off</u>, <u>set off</u>, <u>take off</u>)

A more dramatic change of state is when something explodes. Bombs sometimes go off.

<u>Two-word verb without an object</u> *No problem.*

When we go off something, or somebody, we lose our enthusiasm for it.

I used to like George, but I don't any more. I went off him when I found out about what he did to his wife.

A third meaning of *go off*, almost identical to *be off*, uses off in the *'away from here'* sense.
'I'm going off now.' means *'Goodbye.'* We also say, *'I'm off now.'*
To GO OFF somebody is an <u>inseparable two-word verb</u>
Otherwise, it is a <u>two-word verb without an object</u> No problem in any case.

go on, go on about, go on for

Susanna is very shy and she found it hard to talk in front of the class, but her friends told her to go on, and she finished her speech.

<u>On</u> often means *'continue'* (<u>carry on</u>, <u>get on in years</u>) and *go on* means just that. We often encourage people to continue talking by saying, 'Go on.' It means, 'Don't stop.'

Lazy Maisie never does any work. Her mother is always going on about it, but it doesn't make any difference. Maisie's still lazy.
Lazy Maisie's mother continued to talk about it. (Same as <u>keep on about</u> something.

For often measures duration. So Shy Susanna's speech went on for twenty minutes.

GO ON is a <u>two-word verb without an object</u>. No problem.
GO ON ABOUT is a <u>three-word verb</u>. No problem.
GO ON FOR is a <u>three-word verb</u>. No problem either

go out

When a fire dies, it goes out. We can put out a fire with a bucket of water. It's <u>out</u> now, and we feel the cold, as we often do when we go outdoors.
<u>Two-word verb without an object</u> *No problem.*

go out with

Go out with is romantic. It describes the steady boyfriend or girlfriend. Mary *goes out with* George. They are a couple. Let's hope that they love each other. George and Mary *go out together* - out to the pubs, out to the cinema, out to the bingo. They go <u>out</u> everywhere together.

Contrast this with <u>go in with</u>, which is business.
<u>Three-word verb</u>. *No problem.*

go over

Kenneth was very slow in the general relativity class, and the teacher had to go over it more than once.

<u>Over</u> can have the sense of seeing things from above or from a distance. Think of <u>look over</u> and <u>think over</u>.

Go over a problem means to think about it again, maybe from a fresh angle.
<u>Inseparable two-word verb</u> *No problem.*

139

go through, go through with

To go <u>through</u> something you must be inside it and trying to get outside at the far side.

If you have a lot of work, don't you feel as if you are inside it? This is very similar to *get through* but without the sense of struggle. We also say *run through*, and this is even easier.

Today, I <u>got through</u> a lot of work. (So I'm tired.)
Today, I went through a lot of work. (So I'm happy.)
Today, I <u>ran through</u> a lot of work. (Easy. Do you want me to do more?)
Fat Fat Freddie went through a lot of hamburgers, even though a scientist would say that a lot of hamburgers went through Fat Fat Freddie.
GO THROUGH <u>Inseparable two-word verb</u> No problem.

Sometimes we have to visit the dentist. We sigh. And then we say something like, 'I'll just have to *go through with* it.' We won't enjoy it but we'll do it anyway.
<u>Three-word verb</u> No problem.

go under

This has two meanings. One is exactly the same as <u>come under</u> or <u>fall under</u>. Cats and dogs both go <u>under</u> the heading of

mammals. Mammals go under the heading of vertebrates.
Inseparable two-word verb No problem.

The other meaning is what happened to the Titanic. It sank. It went under. So this is what we say of a bankrupt business.
'What happened to the car dealer on the corner?'
'It went under.'
It went out of business.
Two-word verb without an object No problem.

go up against

While up can have the idea of reaching a limit, against always has the idea of 'confrontation'

Go up against a barrier, a strong obstacle to what you want. A challenge. It is very similar to come up against, but it is more willful, more deliberate.

Hermione wanted to be a policewoman, but she came up against the fact that she was not tall enough. The rules were not going to be changed for her, so she had to give up her dream.

(It was not her intention to challenge the rules.)

But

Big Billy the Bad Boxer went up against the best.

(He did it by choice.) That's why he's so slow now.
Three-word verb. No problem.

go with

To GO WITH someone is a polite expression for spending a whole night with them.
Inseparable two-word verb *No problem.*

go without

'Mum! I want a new computer, and I haven't got the money!'
'What a pity, dear! You'll just have to go without.'
What do poor people do? They go through life without lots of the good things that they would like. They *go without*.
do without means exactly the same.
Inseparable two-word verb, usually without an object.

grow

(grow, grew, grown)
Growing is the natural process of getting bigger.

grow apart

The image is of two plants. When people grow apart it usually means that they slowly stop loving each other. They slowly stop being friends and become indifferent.
Two-word verb without an object *No problem.*

grow out of

Little girls play with dolls. Their older sisters *have grown out of* doing that. They don't play with dolls any more.
Three-word verb. No problem.

grow up

'What do you want to be when you grow up, Gerry?'
'A gangster.'
As normal, <u>up</u> means 'to complete something'. *Grow up* means to *'finish growing'*, to become an adult.
<u>Two-word verb without an object</u>   No problem.

hand
(hand, handed, handed)
We don't use *hand* as a verb on its own. Like <u>put</u> it must have a preposition with it. You hand something somewhere. You pass something somewhere by hand.

hand down

Hand down, like <u>pass down</u>, means to go <u>down</u> through the generations.
You like that Victorian clock? It was handed down to me by my grandmother.
<u>Separable two-word verb</u>   Be careful.

hand out

Typically a teacher will hand photocopies or exercises <u>out</u> to the class. She will make sure that everyone gets one.
<u>Separable two-word verb</u>   Be careful.

hand over

Handing something <u>over</u> from one person to another often implies something of value, something worth buying, stealing, or fighting over.

At eighty years old, I decided to hand over the factory to my sons.
<u>Separable two-word verb</u> Be careful.

hang
(hang, hung, hung)
When we suspend things from a fixed position.
(hang, hanged, hanged)
When we kill people with a rope.

hang on

Here, <u>on</u> has the sense of 'continue' (<u>go on</u>, <u>carry on</u> and so on) In informal English you will often hear the command *'Hang on!'* meaning *'Don't go away!'* Frequently we use it on the phone when we want our victim to wait. We don't want him to <u>hang up</u>.
<u>Two-word verb without an object</u>. No problem.

hang up

A very long time ago telephones had separate mouthpieces and earpieces, and when you finished your call you *hung up* the earpiece. Although, as always, the technology has changed, we still hang up at the end of a phone call.
<u>Two-word verb without an object</u> No problem.

have
(have, had, had)

One of the most important verbs in the language. On its own it can mean possession, sometimes permanent (*I have a Rolls-Royce, I have red hair*) or sometimes temporary (*have a shower, have a drink, have a good time*)

It also used to form the perfect tenses, where it has the basic sense of complete, done, finished.

I have eaten a banana.

(No more banana.)

By next June, we will have been married for 25 years.

(Quarter century done.)

have on

A funny expression. *You're having me on.* It is as if I am a puppet and you are pulling my strings. You have me on a string. You are deceiving me. You are fooling me, making a fool of me.

Did I tell you of the time I wrestled an alligator?

Nah! You're having me on. (I don't believe you.)

Fixed expression.

hold
(hold, held, held)

Hold is to have in your hand. By extension, it is to have something in your control.

Be careful with Mad Mary. She's hearing voices and holding a sword.

hold against

Against always has the idea of 'confrontation'. It is never friendly.

Drusilla is an idiot, but I don't hold it against her.

(I don't hold this fact against her. I don't blame her.)

The idea is that when we blame somebody, we hold the blame in our minds like a weapon that we can use any time against them.

There is a song -

If I told you you have a beautiful body, Would you hold it against me?

It is a separable two-word verb Usually we say 'I don't HOLD it AGAINST him.'

hold down

Holding down a job takes work and effort. If you are too lazy or perhaps too stupid, the job could just fly away. When we talk of someone holding down a job, always there is the sense of achievement. Either the job is very hard or the person is making an effort to better his life.

For ex-prisoners or ex-drug addicts, holding down any job is an achievement.

Separable two-word verb Be careful.

hold on

If you are hanging from a tree, like our

ancestors, it must get very tiring. If you don't *hold on* to the branch, you will fall and possibly die. Sometimes, it takes a lot of strength to hold on.

Mr Johnson had a terrible time trying to keep his fish-and-chips delivery business going. But he held on and he held on, and now he is a success.
<u>Two-word verb without an object</u> No problem.

Our ancestors held on to a branch. Often, we hold on to an idea, a belief or a philosophy.

Corinne was as thin as a lamp-post, but she still held on to the idea that she was fat. Finally, we had to take her to a specialist.
<u>Three-word verb</u>. No problem.

hold out, hold out for

<u>Out</u> is often the opposite of in, and *holding out* is the exact opposite of <u>giving in</u>. When you give in, you surrender, but when you hold out, you resist.

In a tough negotiation, both sides were *holding out for* top dollar. Neither was prepared to give in.
HOLD OUT <u>Two-word verb without an object</u> No problem
HOLD OUT FOR <u>Three-word verb</u> No problem.

hold up

'Why are you HOLDING UP your hands, Mr Sheriff?'

'Because Billy the Kid is pointing a gun at me. This is a hold up.'

By extension, any armed robbery is a *hold up*.

In a hold up, you can't move. By further extension, when you are stuck in a traffic jam, you also can't move. And we say the same thing.

'Where's Miss Bunce? She's usually on time for our meetings.'

'She phoned to say that she is held up in traffic.'

<u>Separable two-word verb</u> Be careful.

join
(joined, joined, joined)

This means to *'put together'* or 'come together in a group'.

join in

You join in a game when you start to play <u>in</u> the game with other people.

Gordon was a strange child who became a strange adult. The other children would never let him join in.

<u>Inseparable two-word verb</u> No problem.

join up

In the old days, <u>up</u> was where the authority was. When you *joined up*, you signed to defend the King against his enemies. You joined the army.

Sign up has the same meaning, and the call up means that you have been *'invited'* to join the forces.
Two-word verb without an object No problem.

keep, keep on
(keep, kept, kept)

To *keep* something is have it in your possession forever.

To *keep doing something* is to continue to do it.

Another variation is to add on, *keep on doing* it. This is similar to carry on

'Why did you hit the defendant?'
'Because he kept on tapping his desk all morning.'

keep ahead

In any race, the person, horse or car in front of the others, is ahead.

If you *keep ahead*, it means that you are ahead in the race, and that you continue to be ahead.

Stay ahead means exactly the same.
Two-word verb without an object No problem.

keep at

Keep means continue and at means to be in contact. When Herbert keeps at something it means the same as keeping on doing.

Horace keeps at his studies all day and most of the night, because he wants to be a psychiatrist. He keeps on studying.
Inseparable two-word verb No problem.

keep in with

Keep in with the right people is easy to understand. It means to stay <u>in</u> their company, to please them. The right people are the people who can help you, which means the rich, the upper class or the well-connected. *Keeping in with* the right people is what social climbers have been doing forever.

<u>Three-word verb</u> No problem.

keep off

<u>Off</u> is the opposite of ON, or it can be a move away from an ON position.

KEEP OFF THE GRASS You might see this sign in a park. You are not on the grass, but don't go on it. Continue not to be on the grass.

'<u>Stay off the grass</u>' means exactly the same.

<u>Inseparable two-word verb</u> No problem.

keep on about

This - the <u>on</u> of continue - means the same as <u>going on about</u> somethng, saying the same thing over and over and over and over and over again.

'Have you heard? Kenny lost all his money in a business opportunity.'
'Yes, we heard. We hear it again and again. He keeps on about it all the time.'
<u>Three-word verb</u> No problem.

You will also hear *'She keeps going on about*

it.' when more emphasis is needed.

keep out, keep out of

There is a sign at an electricity switching room.
Danger of death. KEEP OUT
It means do not go in. You are out of the room, and you must continue to be out of the room.
Stay out means exactly the same.
KEEP OUT is a two-word verb without an object
KEEP OUT OF is a three-word verb. No problem.

keep up, keep up with

Do you remember catch up? If a shoplifter - a thief who steals from shops - runs away, perhaps the store detective will run after him. Maybe he or she is a good runner and can *catch up with* the thief.

You are running a race with an Olympic champion. Perhaps you have a really really good day, and you catch him up. Then your problems have just begun, because now he will get serious. You have to *keep up*. You have to *keep up with* him.

We have a very common expression for the desire to have the same car or better, or the same clothes or better, than our neighbour. This is called *Keeping up with the Jones's*
KEEP UP is a two-word verb without an object. No problem.
KEEP UP WITH is a three-word verb. No problem either.

knock
(knock, knocked, knocked)
To hit something hard with something else hard. You knock on the door with your knuckles or with the heavy metal door-knocker. Unfortunately, knock often means wood against bone. Knocking your head on a low doorway can be painful.

knock about
Old Tony knows everything you need to know about this country. He's been knocking about here for forty years.
The idea here is that Old Tony has had many experiences here, not all of them soft. In fact, one of our expressions for experience is the school of hard knocks. About here means here, there and everywhere.
Knock around means exactly the same.
<u>Inseparable two-word verb</u> *No problem.*

knock off
When you knock something off the shelf, the idea is to take it. Quickly. So knocking something off is to steal it.
'Where are my carpets?'
'They've been knocked of.'.
By extension, a *knock-off* is an illegal copy, like the counterfeit brand-name clothes to pirated films you can buy in the pub. Sometimes it can be an insult for a film that you think copies too exactly the main idea

from someone else. Is *Apocalyse Now* a knock-off of Conrad's *Heart of Darkness*? I will let you decide.
<u>Separable two-word verb</u> *Be careful.*

knock out

<u>Out</u> can often be the conclusion, the end, so that's the end of the boxing match. When someone is knocked out it is similar but rather more violent than when someone passes out
<u>Separable two-word verb</u> *Be careful.*

know
(know, knew, known)

Know is a fantastically difficult philosophical word to define well. But for today let us just say that to know something is to be informed of it. And to know someone means that you have met them before and you remember them.

know about

I know something about quantum mechanics because I studied it for ten years.
<u>Inseparable two-word verb</u> *No problem.*

know of

I know of quantum mechanics. Someone told me in the pub.
<u>Inseparable two-word verb</u> *No problem.*

lay
(lay, laid, laid)

The basic meaning of this word is to *'put something flat on a horizontal surface'*. You can lay a book on the table but you put a cup or a pen on it.

Notice that this verb <u>*always*</u> has an object. You always lay something. Do not confuse it with <u>lie</u> (lie, lay, lain/laid), which never does. Sometimes less-educated natives make this mistake as well.

Happy Harry laid his maps on the table for the geography class.

However,

Lazy Lucinda is always lying on the sofa.

lay off

Sometimes <u>off</u> just means away from here. When you lay something off, you lay it to one side. You stop using it.

By extension, when you *lay people off*, you stop employing them. You do not need them any more. Usually, nowadays, it is not personal. That is to say, people are normally laid off because the business is failing, or the management has decided to close a factory or an office.

The people are laid off and the owners <u>sell off</u> the equipment, the capital.

<u>*Separable two-word verb*</u> *Be careful.*

lay out

You can lay out your plans - literally or not -

on the table. An architect's plans are often called a *lay-out*.

If you sell fruit, at the beginning of the day you lay your fruit out on the counter, at the bar.

Set out can have the same meaning.
Separable two-word verb *Be careful.*

leave
(leave, left, left)

To go away or to abandon. I left Rome last night, but I hope to go back soon. However, I left my phone in the hotel room. Goodbye, phone!

leave out

This is a book for the whole family, so I had to leave out a few verbs that are most definitely phrasal. I had to leave them out of the book. You won't see them here.
Separable two-word verb *Be careful.*

let
(let, let, let)

It means 'to allow', 'to permit' or 'to authorise'.

let down

Penelope thought that Emile was going to marry her, but he let her down.

When somebody breaks their promise to you, you feel let down. You have been allowed to fall. You feel deflated, and your hopes have crashed <u>down</u> to the ground. The person who did this *let you down*.

Mary's aunt promised her a surprise for her birthday. When she got a bar of soap, she felt very let down.

<u>Separable two-word verb</u> . Be careful.

let off

Mrs Barnett was caught stealing bacon from the corner shop, but as it was only her first offence, the magistrate let her off with a warning.

You have been allowed <u>off</u> the hook. (Think about fishing.) You were to have suffered, to be punished, or pay the debt, but you were *let off*. You will not suffer or be punished, and the debt is forgiven.

<u>Separable two-word verb</u> Be careful.

lie

(lie, lay, lain/laid) (The dictionaries will tell you that the past participle is *lain* but I have never heard it. So here you get a choice.)

To stretch yourself horizontally.

Notice that this verb *NEVER* has an object. Do not confuse it with <u>lay</u> (lay, laid, lain/laid) , which always does. Sometimes less-educated natives make this mistake as well.

Lazy Lulu is always lying on the sofa. Yesterday she lay there all day.

But -

Happy Harry laid his maps on the table for

his geography class.

Notice that *lie* (lie, lied, lied) means not to tell the truth.

lie down

Down just makes the idea of *lie* stronger. 'I think I'll go and lie down.' means 'I'm going to lie on my bed for a time.' It is a very popular verb with invalids and old people.
Two-word verb without an object. *No problem.*

lie in

Lie in means to lie in bed in the morning later than usual. Many of our friends lie in on Sundays. It helps make it the best day of the week for busy people.
Two-word verb without an object *No problem.*

live
(live, lived, lived)
What we all do, well or badly. Wise people tell us how to do it, but we forget.

live it down

'Do you remember when Nora was going to Turkey and she took the train to Torquay?' Poor Nora, it will take a long time for her to live it down.
That is, she will have to *live* a long time before her family *calms down* and stops laughing at her.

A humiliation or an embarrassment makes the blood rush up to your face. And if the embarrassment is acute, your family and friends will happily remember it forever.
Separable two-word verb Usually a fixed expression.

live off

We sometimes use off for the sense of separation.

A farmer lives off his land. That is, he lives by taking the wealth, the good things off the land. Parasites live off their hosts. Certain kinds of criminals live off *'immoral earnings'*, which is to say, off ladies-to-rent. The owner of a block of flats lives off the rents.
Inseparable two-word verb No problem.

live together

To *live together* is for two people to live as if they were married, but without any official or church ceremony.

Two people who live together also live with each other.
Two-word verb without an object No problem.

live it up

Sometimes up is the world of fantasy and imagination.

Living it up means spending lots of money, having parties every night, driving wonderful cars too fast, having servants to help you with the boring things of life, and

so on.
Fixed expression.

live up to

The TV presenter says, 'And I am very happy to welcome here tonight the best, the most talented, the funniest and most amazing performer it has ever been my pleasure to introduce...'
'How can I live up to that?'

Up is a high standard. When we live up to a fine reputation, or a high moral standard, we may find it very difficult.
Three-word verb No problem.

live with

To live with somebody is to live together as if you were married, but without any official or church ceremony.
Two people who *live with* each other live together.
Inseparable two-word verb No problem.

look
(look, looked, looked)

What you do with your eyes with intention. It also has a second meaning of 'appear'.
I looked at Marilyn Monroe. She looked wonderful.

look about, look around, look round

These all mean exactly the same.
How many times in your life have you had the following conversation in a shop?
'Can I help you?'
'No thanks. I'm just looking round.'
One of the most common meanings of about is 'from here to there to somewhere else'.
Round in many verbs means 'approximately here' or 'here, but not urgently' So, *'look in the shop'* is direct, but *'look round the shop'* is more relaxed.
Inseparable two-word verbs. No problem.

look after

Not long ago, childbirth was dangerous, and many mothers lost their lives. If somebody looked at a new-born baby after the mother's death, they had the responsibility to care for the child. They pledged to *look after it*.
To look after anybody is to take care of them.
Inseparable two-word verb No problem.

look ahead

It is very difficult to sell pension plans to teenagers. They don't want to look ahead to when they are old.
To *look ahead* is to look forward in time. When I look ahead, I am trying to look in

the direction I am going. I am trying to predict the future. I am trying to plan.
<u>Two-word verb without an object</u> No problem.

look back, look back at, look back on, look back to

<u>Back</u>, after a verb, nearly always has the sense of *'return'*

When we look back, we are remembering the past, often with affection.

Hilary looked back to her time in school. 'Oh,' she said. 'Were my schooldays the happiest days of my life?'

LOOK BACK AT,
LOOK BACK ON,
LOOK BACK TO all mean exactly the same.

LOOK BACK *is a <u>two-word verb without an object</u>   No problem.*
LOOK BACK AT, LOOK BACK ON, LOOK BACK TO are <u>three-word verbs</u>. No problem either..

look down on

Many, many years ago in Europe there were only three kinds of people: those who fought, those who worked, and those who prayed. The best people, the lords and ladies, all rode about their land on horseback. And frequently they would see their peasants, on foot, <u>down</u> in the fields, working hard. The best people then, like the best people now, despised everyone else. They literally *looked down on* them.

The poor peasants, full of respect, (the lord always had his sword) would literally look up to him.

Mohammed Ali wants this on his gravestone
HE NEVER LOOKED DOWN ON THOSE WHO LOOKED UP TO HIM
Three-word verb No problem.

look for

Elizabeth is looking for a husband. She wants to get married before she is thirty.
One of the commonest meanings of for is the reason why you do something. When you *look for* something, you are looking in order to find it. You are searching. And that is exactly what it means. It is very different from watch for.
Inseparable two-word verb No problem.

look forward to

Every December our children look forward to Christmas very much.
Look forward clearly means looking in the direction you are going, but that is not the whole story. It is never used literally. We use it in the sense of expectation, anticipation, and it is *only* optimistic. We only look forward to pleasure.
They're looking forward to opening their presents from Santa Claus.
Nobody looks forward to going to the dentist.

Grammar note

LOOK FORWARD TO SOMETHING and LOOK FORWARD TO DOING SOMETHING. Notice that TO followed by a -ING form is rare in English. It will be in your next exam.
Three-word verb. No problem.

look into

It was apparently a sad suicide, but when Sherlock Holmes looked into the matter, it was clear that it was a case of murder.
When you look into something, it means to *look* carefully *into* it, to investigate it.
Inseparable two-word verb No problem.

look out, look out for

On a ship a long time ago, before satellites and so forth, there was a man high up on the main mast whose job was to *look out* over the sea. He was the look-out. He was looking out for land and for danger.

Now, when someone shouts, *'LOOK OUT!'* prepare for danger **NOW!**

'Look out! We're going to have an accident!'
'If you don't look out, the boss will fire you.'
'My mum says if I don't look out, I'll fail my exams.'
When you cross this street, look out for bad drivers.

Watch out is similar but usually less urgent.
LOOK OUT Two-word verb without an object No problem.
LOOK OUT FOR Three-word verb No problem.

look over
You look <u>over</u> a landscape from a high place like a mountain or a balloon. You can see the big picture but not the details. When you look over a problem, you are doing the same thing.

Hetty hated maths. Every time she looked over her homework, she would go into a dream.
<u>Inseparable two-word verb</u> No problem.

look through
Apart from the obvious idea of looking through a telescope, we use this for quickly reading <u>through</u> - in the sense of being *in* the experience of - a magazine without really reading it. It's similar to <u>go through</u>, but with less effort.

At the hairdresser's, Mrs Arkwright used to look through the society magazines. She didn't read them, of course. She just looked at the photos and discussed high society gossip with her friends.
<u>Inseparable two-word verb</u> No problem.

look up
In the old days, reference books and holy books were big, heavy things that were really valuable. There were often chained on special stands, so that thieves couldn't take them. You had to stand <u>up</u> to consult them. To find anything in a book like this, you had

to *look up* the information. You had to *look it up*.
Now we use this to mean 'search for information' in any reference book, such as dictionaries, encyclopaedias, phone books, bus timetables, and so on. It is why you use Google.

'What's the capital of Burkina Faso?'
'Look it up.'
<u>Separable two-word verb</u> *Be careful.*

look up to

Many many years ago there were only three kinds of people: those who fought, those who worked, and those who prayed. The best people, the kings and lords and ladies, all rode about their land on horseback. And frequently they would see their peasants, on foot, working hard.
The poor peasants would, literally, *look up to* them. <u>Up</u> to the lords and ladies.

Mohammed Ali wants this on his gravestone
HE NEVER <u>LOOKED DOWN ON</u> THOSE WHO LOOKED UP TO HIM
<u>Three-word verb</u> *No problem.*

make
(make, made, made)
The basic meaning of this word is *'to create'*.

make for

It starts to rain hard. Somebody in the group shouts, 'Make for the trees.' And we all run towards the trees.

This is short for *'make (a straight line) for the trees.'*

MAKE FOR is an <u>inseparable two-word verb</u> and has to be followed by a place.
MAKE FOR somewhere. No problem.

make out

'Someone left a message on my voicemail, but I couldn't make it out.'

I am looking at shapes in a fog. What are they? I can't <u>make</u> a picture in my mind that corresponds to what I see out there. I can't *make out* the people. It's impossible to *make them out.*

'Juana is a very strange woman. I can't make her out.'

(I don't understand her.)

<u>Separable two-word verb</u>   Be careful.

make up

One of the meanings of <u>up</u> is *'to a higher standard'* and so, of course, when a woman makes her face up to a higher standard - to be more beautiful - she *makes up*. She puts on *make-up*. All of this can be a great mystery for men.

In this sense, MAKE UP is a <u>two-word verb without an object</u>

Sometimes, the real world can be a little dull and boring, so we have to invent

something. We have to make something up to a higher standard, to be a bit more exciting. In other words, we invent a story.
'Don't believe anything that Amaryllis says. She's always making things up.'
This MAKE UP is a <u>separable two-word verb</u> Be careful.

Yet another way we use *make up* is the sense of compensating for a bad time. After a quarrel, lovers often make up. If they don't, they are no longer lovers. Again, <u>up</u> here means a higher standard.
<u>Two-word verb without an object</u> No problem.

A common expression when somebody borrows something from you or steals your time is *'Don't worry. I'll make it up to you.'* (I will compensate you.)
Fixed expression, but notice that with this meaning it is a <u>separable three-word verb</u>.

make up for

'Dalmatia is not very pretty, but she makes up for it with her charm and her brains.'
We have to make something <u>up</u> to a higher standard for a reason.
A shy person who has difficulty in meeting new people might <u>make</u> her behaviour *up* to a higher standard <u>for</u> the reason of her timidity. She could become very noisy, for example, drink too much, or be too generous. She *makes up for* her shyness. She compensates for her shyness by being noisy.

Make up for means to compensate for something.
Three-word verb No problem.

make up to

This has a completely different meaning from make it up to you.. The idea is being nice to people who are higher up than you.
'He is always making up to the president's secretary.'
Another way of saying this is
'He is always kissing up to the president's secretary.'
There are yet other less polite expressions, but not in this book.
Three-word verb No problem.

mix
(mix, mixed, mixed)

You put water and wine into the same glass at the same time you are mixing them. Once things are mixed it is very difficult to separate them again.

mix up

To mix completely (up) Be extension, we say that someone or something is mixed up when they are confused.
'Tomasina is a bit mixed up. She married the wrong man. Twice.'
Separable two-word verb Be careful.

move

(move, moved, moved)
The act of going from one place to another.

move in, move out

Move often has the sense of move where you live, to move house. When someone *moves in*, they come to live with you, in the same house. And *move out* is the opposite. When they go out of the house for the last time - when they leave you.

move to has the same sense of moving house.
Two-word verb without an object. No problem.

move off

Sometimes off means *'away from here'*. Such as go off on a journey, or set off on another journey. We use *move off* to emphasise the movement itself. For example, when a ship leaves the dock.
Two-word verb without an object No problem.

move over

Sometimes over has the sense *'from one side to the other'*. Such as pass over (to the world to come) or put over an idea from one mind to another.

Move over is more mundane. You sit crowded on a bench seat on the bus or the metro. 'Move over,' says Mr Fatte. 'I need more space.'

move up has the same meaning.
Two-word verb without an object No problem.

move to
Move frequently has the sense of move where you live, to move house.
'What happened to Gerald?'
'Didn't you hear? He moved to Berlin. He got the job he wanted.'
move in and move out have the same sense of moving home.
Inseparable two-word verb No problem.

move up
As in come up to a fence, or to go up against a strong enemy, up can have the idea of reaching a limit
I was sitting on a seat on the metro. 'Move up,' said Mr Fatte. 'I need space.'
move over has the same meaning here.
A similar meaning is when an army *moves* its forces *up* to the front.
Separable two-word verb Problem.

name
(name, named, named)
To name something is to give it a name.

name after
Perhaps you were *named after* your grandmother. You have the same name, but she had it first. Usually, after means later in

time. From time to time a baby in England gets eleven names. He is named after the players in his Dad's favourite football team.
Call after means exactly the same..
Notice the similarity with take after.
name for has the same meaning.
Inseparable two-word verb No problem.

name for

One thing or person can be in the place of, a second one. That is to say, one thing for another.
You were named for one of your mother's heros. You have the same name, but the hero had it first.
name after means the same.
Inseparable two-word verb No problem.

own

(own, owned, owned)
To have, or to possess, in a legal sense. That car belongs to me. I am the owner. And I have the documents to prove it.

own up to

Up is the direction of Heaven and authority. (Compare give up, sign up.)
To own something is to take responsibility for it.
When you *own up to* something, you take the responsibility for it before Authority. In other words, you confess.

'All right,' said Miss Harmony the music teacher. 'Own up! Who put detergent in the saxophones?'
<u>Three-word verb</u> *No problems.*

pass
(pass, passed, passed)
To move in relation to something else that is not moving. Time passes. Mr George passes this way every afternoon at half past three.

pass away, pass on, pass over
All of these are polite expressions meaning *'to die'*. The soul passes <u>on</u> to a new life. It passes <u>over</u> to the other side.
<u>Away</u> means you never see them again
<u>Two-word verb without an object</u> *No problem.*

pass down
Things pass down through time. Most wall calendars go <u>down</u> from the past to the present and further down to the future. Valuable things tend to pass down through the generations.
Grandad passed down his watch to me. He left it to me in his will.
<u>Separable two-word verb</u> *Be careful.*

pass for
Fran the Fan Dancer is 36, but in a low light she can pass for 16.

172

Something that can *pass* through life <u>for</u>, in the sense of *'instead of'*, something else.
These new forgeries are very good. They pass for good notes nearly everywhere.
<u>Separable two-word verb</u>   Problem.

pass off

To pass something off, is to *pass* something false <u>off</u> your hands as if it were real.
Fitz the Forger is wonderful. He makes beautiful copies of banknotes. You can pass them off anywhere.
This means the same as
Fitz's notes can <u>pass for</u> genuine notes in any bank.
<u>Separable two-word verb</u>   Take care.

pass out

When you lose consciousness, when you faint, you pass <u>out</u> of the everyday world. You *pass out*.
<u>Two-word verb without an object</u> No problem.

pass up

To pass something <u>up</u> to Heaven is to renounce it. It is similar to <u>give up</u>, but without the sense of sacrifice. You *pass up* an opportunity that you don't particularly care about
I often get invitations in the post to play lotteries of foreign countries. I find it really easy to pass up these chances. The invitations go straight into the bin.
<u>Separable two-word verb</u>   Careful.

pick, pick up
(pick, picked, picked)

We pick fruit when we take it from the tree. When we *pick* apples from the apple tree, there is an idea of selection, and, by extension, pick can also mean 'select'

Maradona was picked for Argentina, again.

We also *pick up* a pencil from a table, for example

Sam went to China for a year, but he only picked up a few words of Chinese.

PICK UP is a separable two-word verb. Be careful.

pick off

Off often means a change of state or position. Milk can go off, or somebody can set off a firework.

Imagine a row of little birds flying in a line in a video game. Harry the Video Hunter *picks* them *off*, one by one. That is, he shoots first one, then another, then another.......

(Real birds are not so stupid, of course.)

Separable two-word verb. Careful.

pick on

Here, pick has the sense of 'select'. And on sometimes can be aggressive. (When somebody is literally *on* something else, it is in a superior position. It can dominate. Think of wrestling.) Look at turn on somebody, and having the guard dog set on a burglar.

When hooligans pick on somebody, they have selected him for a bad time.

<u>Inseparable two-word verb</u> No problem.

pick out

In a normal crowd, it's really easy to pick out the basketball players. They stand head and shoulders over the rest. (It is simple to distinguish them. They <u>stand out</u>.) One of the meanings of pick is *'to select'*, and *pick out* emphasises this idea further. We pick <u>out</u> something from the crowd.

<u>Separable two-word verb</u> Be careful.

pick up

Not only can you pick <u>up</u> a book that has fallen on the floor, or pick up a language after living in a country for a year or two, you can also pick up a disease from being in the wrong place, pick up your friend from the station, or pick up (the thread of) a half-forgotten conversation.

'Let's pick up where we left off.'

You can also pick up a new romantic friend in a bar or a club where there is lots of dancing.

<u>Separable two-word verb</u> Be careful.

pick up on

My English teacher is always picking up on my mistakes. I hate her.

By extension from <u>pick up</u>, *pick up on*

means to detect.
As Detective Jones was talking to Milly Molly, he picked up on the fact that something was not right. She knew more than she was saying.
Three-word verb No problem

play
(play, played, played)
Play is what children do when they are not at school. They play in the house, in the street, in the park. They play everywhere. And it is fun. This is always contrasted to work, which is serious.
Musicians also play their instruments.

play at
She went to the United States to learn English but after a year she didn't even know the plural of 'woman'. She was only playing at learning the language..
Play is always contrasted to work, which is serious. So to play at something, is to do it but not seriously. It is a contemptuous expression.
Inseparable two-word verb No problem.

play back
Back, after a verb, almost always has the sense of *'return'*
Musicians play their instruments and so, by extension, do recording machines, CD systems, and so on. Once the music has

been recorded, you want to hear it again, don't you? Then the machine *plays it back* to you.
<u>Separable two-word verb</u> Careful.

play down

Yvette lost all her hearing in her left ear, but she plays it down. She doesn't talk about it, and you never notice.

When we <u>turn down</u> the music, we make it less loud. We make it quieter.

By extension, we can *play* a situation like an instrument and when we *play* the situation <u>down</u>, we make it less important. We take the emphasis away from it.
<u>Separable two-word verb</u> . Careful.

play up

Mr Wellington was a successful politician who always knew how to play up the mistakes of his enemies. Every time they said something wrong, he let everyone know.

When we <u>turn up</u> the music, we make it louder.

By extension, we can play a situation like an instrument and when we *play* the situation <u>up</u>, we make it more important. We give it more emphasis.
<u>Separable two-word verb</u> . Careful.

point

(point, pointed, pointed)
To indicate with the point of your finger.

Notice that point <u>to</u> something is not quite the same as to point <u>at</u> it.

At can be aggressive so we usually say point at people.

'Don't point at the strange man, Jeremy. It's not his fault.'

Some of us were told as children that it was rude to point at somebody.

The dial on your car points to 100 miles an hour (about 160 km) and you hear the police.

The importance of the situation, said the business manager in the fourth meeting, points to an immediate search for a solution

POINT AT, POINT TO <u>Inseparable two-word verbs</u>.

point out

'The idea in boxing,' said the champ, 'is to hurt him more than he hurts me. I just wanted to point that out.'

(He just wanted to indicate it <u>out</u> to the world.)

<u>Separable two-word verb</u>   Be careful.

pull
(pull, pulled, pulled)

This is when you move something a little heavy or difficult towards you. It is the opposite of <u>push</u>.

pull ahead

In any race, the person, horse or car in front of the others, is <u>ahead</u>. Think of <u>get ahead</u> or

stay ahead.
Maybe the horse race is very close with no clear winner yet, but now Mighty Wonder is pulling ahead of the rest.
It is as if he was pulling the winning post towards him. This means exactly the same as push ahead.

Two-word verb without an object No problem.

pull away

Pull away means exactly the same as pull ahead. If you watch horse racing you will hear this a lot. (By the way, listening to horse racing is a wonderful idea for improving your listening in general. The commentators talk really really fast. Ten minutes is worth an hour of an action film with explosions, for example. And if you put money on it, it will keep your attention.)

Two-word verb without an object No problem.

pull back

Back, after a verb, almost always has the sense of 'return'
An army pulls back to its previous position. It retreats. The general is pulling his army back to its previous position.

Usually a two-word verb without an object, so no problem. But it can be a separable two-word verb

pull off

Off frequently means a change of state or position (like go off, take off). When you

pull something off, you have taken it away.
By extension, when you pull off a project, you also complete it. When do you complete a project? When it is finished.
When you *pull off* a project, it is a success. Always.
Compare this with bring off and carry off.
Also, a project can come off.
They all mean exactly the same.
Daisy pulls it off.
Daisy succeeds in something difficult. Well done, Daisy!
Usually a fixed expression. Separable two-word verb *Be careful.*

pull through

The doctors told us that she could die, but she pulled through.
Through means movement from outside something, in to it, and then outside it again. Often this is difficult. For example - break through, get through something, and think through a hard problem..
Pull through is a crisis. If you pull through an illness, it means that you survive it. It didn't kill you. Something - or Someone - is pulling you through this crisis.
Two-word verb without an object *No problem.*

push
(push, pushed, pushed)
This is when you move something a little heavy or difficult away from you. It is the

opposite of pull.

push ahead

In any race, the person, horse or car in front of the others, is ahead. Think of get ahead or stay ahead.

Maybe the race is very close with no clear winner yet, but now Mighty Wonder is pushing ahead of the rest.

It is as if he is making a special effort pushing against the ground

It means exactly the same as pull ahead.

<u>Two-word verb without an object</u> No problem.

push around

If you put big boys and little boys together in the same playground, the little ones soon get pushed around.

If you can *push somebody around* the place, he or she is weak and easy to dominate. (This person is also known as a *'pushover'*.)

<u>Separable two-word verb</u> Careful.

push for

One of the commonest meanings of for is a reason to do something. Such as go for, look for, or stand for for Parliament.

If you work in a big organisation, and you want something important to happen, you want something done, you have to *push for* it. You have to *push* through much resistance (also known as your colleagues

and your boss) *for* your project.
<u>Inseparable two-word verb</u> *No problem.*

push off
This is an inelegant way of telling somebody to go away. There are other, ruder, ways of saying the same thing using taboo verbs and <u>off</u>. But not in this book.
Fixed expression. No problem.

put
(put, put, put)
Put means *'to place'*, *'to position'*. It must *always* have a preposition after it. You put something somewhere. Otherwise it makes no sense.

put about, put around
<u>About</u> often means 'here, there, everywhere'.
To *put it about* is to place something here, there, and who knows where else. The *it* means a piece of news, a tasty scandal, something the speaker disapproves of. To put it about means to spread gossip.
After Mary the gossip put it about that he had once been in prison, George was not welcome anywhere in the village.
<u>Separable two-word verb</u> . *Be careful.*

put across
I used to hate maths, until the new teacher, Mr Marsden, arrived. He puts it all across

so well. I can understand it now.
To *put something across* means to put some information, a new idea perhaps, across an imaginary table. *'To put something across well'* means *'to successfully communicate it'*.
The defence lawyer put his case across so well that the jury believed him, so O J Simpson went free.
Put over has the same meaning. Compare this with get across, and get over.
Separable two-word verb Be careful.

put away, put aside, put by

Away is not here, *aside* means *'to one side'* and *by* means *'near'* or *'close'*.
To have some money *put away, put aside* or *put by* means to have some money saved in a bank, put under the bed, or in a dirty old sock.
set aside means exactly the same.

But, *put away* has another, less friendly meaning.
Jimmy's uncle was put away for seven years.
It means that he is in prison. The Law put him away.
Separable two-word verbs. Be careful.

put down

Georgina was an intelligent girl with no

friends. She was always putting people down.

To put somebody down means to publicly place someone down in a lower position. Therefore it means to humiliate them, despise them, or just to speak badly about them.

<u>Separable two-word verb</u> *Be careful.*

put (the dog) down

This is a euphemism. When your dog is very old or ill, and it is time for him to go to the doghouse in the sky, you can take him to the vet, and the vet will kill him.

<u>Separable two-word verb</u> *Be careful.*

put it down to

When we don't understand something, it feels vague and confusing, as if it is smoke or vapour that we can't catch. But once we do understand it, that is a different story. It is now nailed down to the floor. It's solid. We have an explanation, and it feels familiar and safe.

Isn't it true that Freud puts everything down to childhood experience?

Must have an object between PUT and DOWN. <u>It is a rare separable three-word verb.</u> *Be careful.*

put forward

At a meeting in the Town Hall, the Majority Party put several proposals forward designed to win the next election.

The Opposition Party stated that this was an insult to the people, and put forward some counter-proposals of their own.

Sometimes it has a rather formal sense, like come forward.

Forward is the direction in which we normally go.

To *put something forward* is similar to put something across in the sense that what you put forward is information, or an idea. To put an idea forward is to formally propose it in a meeting it.

Separable two-word verb . Be careful.

put off

Penelope has had nine months to prepare for this exam, but she kept putting it off and putting it off, so that now she only has one week to study.

We say off when we mean *'away from this situation'* or *'away from here'* so, by extension, it can mean *'away from now'* into the future. So to put something off means *'to postpone it'*

'Why have we got water in the kitchen?'
'Because your dad told me he was going to mend the roof, but he kept putting it off.'

Separable two-word verb Be careful.

put off

Vernon thought that he was a ladies man, but he only talked about himself. This put the girls off completely.

As so often, off here has the idea of 'away from this situation' or 'away from here'. So, to *put somebody off* means to make people lose enthusiasm for an idea.

'I ordered fried eggs on toast, but the eggs were almost green. That put me off.'

This happened to me and, yes, it did put me off.

turn off can have the same meaning.

Separable two-word verb . *Be careful.*

put on

You put on your clothes most mornings (and at night you take them off). Who puts on different clothes most often? Actors. In the past, satirical actors, above all, put on masks. (Satire could be a little dangerous in the old days. Laughing at the lord with his sword had its own risks.)

By extension, when you are *putting someone on*, you are mocking them. You are laughing at them with a satire. When you are in England, please note that the English love irony and satire, and may well be putting you on without your knowledge.

Separable two-word verb Be careful.

put out

A noted English writer died in the trenches of the First World War. His famous last words were, *'Put that ****** cigarette out!'*

When fires die, they go out. When we extinguish a fire, we put it out. It's out now,

and we feel the cold, as we often do when we go outdoors.
Separable two-word verb . Be careful.

put over

I used to hate econometrics until the new teacher, Mrs Gladiola, arrived. She puts it over so well. I can understand it now.

To put something over means to put some information, some valuable teaching, over an imaginary table. *'To put something over well'* means *'to successfully communicate it'*.

Put across has the same meaning. Compare this with get across and get over.
Separable two-word verb Be careful.

There is also an expression.
George put one over on you.
He fooled you. He made a fool of you. He lied and you believed it. Ha ha ha, more fool you!

put through

Through means 'outside, then inside, then outside again'. Light comes through the window. It is outside the window, then (for a picosecond) it is inside the glass, and then it is outside the glass again. Trains go from England to France through a tunnel.

Like put across and put forward, it is information that is moved. We imagine a cable or a phone line as a pipe. Electricity or

information goes through the cable.
In the old days when you phoned somebody in a company you had to go through the switchboard. You had to speak to the lady and persuade her to connect you to the person you wanted. When that happened she would say, *'Putting you through.'*
When this had happened you had got through. You had got through to the person you wanted.
Separable two-word verb . Be careful.

put up
When good friends of yours come to stay for a long weekend, you don't send them off to a hotel. That is no way to keep your friends. No, you put up a temporary bed - maybe a camp bed. By extension, we say that you put up your friends for the weekend.
It means 'to provide free accommodation'
Separable two-word verb   Be careful.

put up with
Kate's husband is so rude and abusive all the time. I don't how she puts up with it.
Put something up on your shoulder means to carry it, to accept responsibility for it, to tolerate it. It is a burden, but you shoulder it. You put up with it.
No, I don't like paying my mortgage every month. But what can you do? I put up with it.
Three-word verb No problem.

put upon

Upon is an older version of *on*. (Look at it. Originally it was *up on*.) You put something on something else.

Sometimes his boss puts a great load upon poor Maurice's shoulders. He feels like a victim. He feels very put upon.
Nearly always we use this verb in the passive.

rule
(rule, ruled, ruled)

There are two meanings of rule. One is that what the traditional king does, what the boss does. Although in modern monarchies, it is a little more subtle. The king or queen reigns, but parliament rules. But for today, let's the say the king rules.

The other ruler is a device with straight edges that we all know for making straight lines on paper. You rule a straight line with it.

rule out

When you rule (because you are the ruler), you can rule something out. You can exclude it. It is <u>out</u> of here. Or ...
With your ruler on the desk you can draw a line through some words. You rule them out, which is the same as <u>crossing them out</u>. You choose.
<u>Separable two-word verb</u>   *Be careful.*

run
(run, ran, run)
How you move fast without technology.
It can also mean *'flow'*. A river runs.
A third meaning is when we run something. We make it flow, as it were. A manager runs a company, or a shop, or a factory. Civil servants run the country, perhaps.

run across

When you *run across* somebody, you collide with them by accident, usually not literally. Expressed more politely, you meet that person by chance. run into has the same meaning.
I ran across Mr Sebastian today in the supermarket. He looked very happy because someone bought his house at last.
Run into means exactly the same.
<u>Inseparable two-word verb</u> No problem.

run away

When you run away, you *run away* from somewhere, usually quickly, because it is bad there. People who run away from situations too easily are never respected.
<u>Two-word verb without an object</u> No problem.

run down

In the old days, most clocks ran by mechanisms - called clockwork - that needed winding up. If you were too lazy or forgetful to wind the clock up, it *ran down*. By extension, if somebody looks like he is tired and a little ill, we say that he, too, is *run down*.

run for, stand for

In the United States, when an ambitious person wants to be a politician, he or she *runs for* election. In Britain, a would-be politician stands for election. What does that tell you about the two different countries?

One of the commonest meanings of for is the reason why you do something.

Inseparable two-word verb No problem.

run into

When you *run into* somebody, you crash into them by accident, usually not literally. Expressed more politely, you meet that person by chance. run across means the same.

I ran into Mrs Armand today in the post-office. She told me that her life was full of stress these days.

Run across means exactly the same.

Inseparable two-word verb No problem.

run out, run out of

Sugar *runs out of* the bag. Water runs out of the jug. And beer runs out of the barrel.

When they are all empty, the sugar, the

water, and the beer have *run out*.

By extension, we have *run out of* sugar, water, and beer. There is none left.

Desmond the Politician lies all the time, so nobody believes him any more. He's run out of credibility.

RUN OUT *is a* two-word verb without an object *No problem.*
RUN OUT OF *is a* three-word verb. *No problem either.*

run over

This is violent. When you *run over* someone, you do it with your car. This, of course, can be fatal. Once I heard a child scream, *'I'll get my Dad to run over your head.'*

Separable two-word verb *Be careful.*

run through

To run through something you must be inside it and trying to get outside to the far side. Trains go <u>through</u> a tunnel, and planes fly through the air.

If you have a lot of work, don't you feel as if you are inside it?

This is very similar to get through and go through but without the sense of struggle.

Today, I *got through* a lot of work.   (So I'm tired.)

Today, I *went through* a lot of work.   (So I'm happy.)

Today, I *ran through* a lot of work.   (Easy. Do want me to do more?)

Inseparable two-word verb *No problem.*

run up

Running through a lot of work is easy. So, unfortunately for lots of us, is running up a big bill. Invite all the pretty ladies to bottles of champagne. No problem, just put it on the bill.
Separable two-word verb Be careful.

see
(see, saw, seen)
What we do with our eyes and much of our brains.

see about

To *see about* something means to see that something gets done, that a problem is solved. It is very similar to see to but there is less determination. *'I will see about the problem of recruitment in our Birmingham office.'* means *'I will give this problem my attention for about ten minutes a day.'*
Inseparable two-word verb No problem.

see in

There are two common expressions. One is what every girl's girlfriends have said about her new boyfriend.
'I don't know what she sees in him.'
They can't see his good qualities, what is in him.
Inseparable two-word verb with this meaning. No problem.

The other meaning is similar to see out and see it through. Every year we *see in* the New Year with a celebration.
Separable two-word verb with this meaning. Like SEE OUT. Be careful.

see off

You see your friend off (from his visit, perhaps) when you escort him to the station. *'Goodbye, friend. Come back soon.'*
There is also a similar but less friendly meaning.
Imagine that you own a nice piece of land. You also have a large dog - called Ugly Mug - that never has enough to eat.
One day, some strange visitors arrive, and they try to interest you in their philosophy. You politely ask them to leave, but they don't.
'Hey, Ugly Mug,' you say to the dog. *'See them off.'* And Ugly Mug sees them off the land. He *sees* that the unwelcome visitors are *off* his land.
Separable two-word verb . Be careful.

see out

Out here means the end.
Magda came into a lot of money and she decided to buy some good furniture for a change. When I went to see her, I had to admire her new solid dining table. 'It will last for centuries,' she said. 'It will see me out.'

The table will '*see*' her *out* of this life.
<u>Separable two-word verb</u> *Be careful.*

see through, see it through

When you see <u>through</u> a project, it is like <u>going through</u> it, but often with the sense of supervising it, guiding it, or managing it. When you have seen it through, you have finished it.
'We're late on the Birmingham project.'
'I know there's been some problems, but I'm seeing it through.'
I take responsibility for finishing it.
<u>Separable two-word verb</u> *Be careful.*

see through, see through it

Normally we can see through a window because it is transparent. And if you lie to me and you are bad at lying, I can see <u>through</u> your story. You have not deceived me, not fooled me. You have not made a fool of me.
<u>Inseparable two-word verb</u> *No problem.*

see to

See to something means to see that something gets done, that a problem is solved. 'I will see to the problem of falling sales in our Inverness branch.' means 'I will give this problem my full attention.'

Don Ferrari has a problem with a competitor. His assistant says, 'Don't worry, boss. I'll see to it.' And the boss has a competitor less.

see about is similar, but with less commitment.

Inseparable two-word verb No problem.

sell

(sell, sold, sold. Like *tell*, *told*, *told*.)
What you do when you exchange something you have, or something you do, for money.

sell by

In time, by means *'at or before'* It is a deadline.
So *'sell by January 2020'* means that the item must be sold on or before January 2020.

Separable two-word verb Careful.

sell off

Sometimes off it just means away from here. When you lay something off, you lay it to one side. You stop using it.

Owners normally lay off employees because the business is failing, or because the management has decided to close a factory or an office. When this happens, the capital equipment of the factory, the factory itself, is *sold off*.

Separable two-word verb . *Be careful.*

sell out

SOLD OUT means that there is nothing left. You go to buy a couple of tickets for the new Holly Wood film, but they have *sold out*. So you have to do something else that night. Compare this with run out.
When we say somebody has sold out, it also means that there is nothing left. That is to say, that he has *sold* his trust, his integrity, his honour, *out* for money or for fame. In other words, he has been corrupted.
Fixed expression. No problem.
By extension, to *sell somebody out* is to betray them. Think of Judas and the thirty pieces of silver.
Separable two-word verb . *Be careful.*

sell up

Very often up has the sense of 'complete' or 'finish' so when you *sell up*, you sell everything you have into cash and start again, often in a new town, or even a new country.
Two-word verb without an object *No problem.*

send
(send, sent, sent)

To send is to transmit. It can be a thing, it can be a message, or it can be information. You send something from one place to another.

send back

Back means return as nearly always.
I am at a restaurant with my favourite person. She looks at what the waiter has brought and says to me, 'That's not what I ordered.' 'Fine,' I say. 'Let's send it back.' And back to the kitchen it goes.
<u>Separable two-word verb</u> Be careful.

send down

Literally, you send somebody <u>down</u> from a high place to a lower one. There are two common uses that I know, where 'high' and 'low' have a social meaning, not a physical one.

Students at Oxford or Cambridge - the two most prestigious universities in Britain - could be *sent down* if they were no good. They were expelled, ejected, kicked out, asked to leave.

'What happened to Harry?'
'Sent down for ten years.'
He will be in prison for ten years.
Usually passive. TO BE SENT DOWN.

send up

On television there is a programme* of plastic puppets that send up the politicians of the country. The programme is much more popular than the politicians themselves.
*'programme' is British English. The Americans write 'program'.

Before the Wright brothers it was very difficult to send up anything. You could only send up a balloon, which is a ridiculous, inflated, pompous thing. In fact, even the thought of it was so difficult that it was ridiculous. And that is the idea that has continued with us.

To send somebody up is to imitate them in a ridiculous, funny, or sarcastic way.

<u>Separable two-word verb</u> . *Be careful.*

set
(set, set, set)

First, you have to have some idea what *set* means. It means, approximately, moving or changing something in such a way that it is difficult to move or change it back. It is something that is difficult to undo. When lovely wet, sticky concrete is left, it dries and becomes hard, and no amount of water will turn hard concrete soft. The concrete sets.

Old Harry is set in his ways. He doesn't want to learn anything any more. He says, 'You can't teach an old dog new tricks.'

When you change your clocks at the beginning or the end of summer, you set your clocks. You *set them <u>forward</u>* in the spring, and in the autumn you *set them <u>back</u>*.

set about

Joe's carpet business was going downhill,

until his wife took charge and set about improving it. She had to work very hard but now it's doing fine.

To *set about* a task or a project is to start doing it seriously. The idea of *set*, as always, has a sense of permanence.

<u>Inseparable two-word verb</u> You SET ABOUT a job, or you SET ABOUT doing a job. No problem.

set after

Hey, Wally's gone to the airport, but he's forgotten his passport. If you set after him now, you should get to the airport on time.

<u>Set out</u> and <u>set off</u> both mean to start a journey. And <u>after</u> means later in time or in a sequence, like go after or name after.

When you *set after somebody*, it means to <u>set out</u> or <u>set off</u> on a journey *after* the person. You hope that you can <u>catch up with</u> him.

Set after is less aggressive than <u>go after</u>. It does not suggest hunting or killing.

<u>Inseparable two-word verb</u> No problem.

set against

Agatha wanted to go to university but her father was set against it, so she started work as a hairdresser.

<u>Against</u> always has the idea of 'confrontation'

Nearly always used in the passive, to be *set against something* means to be determined against it. Remember that set means

'difficult to undo'.
Fixed expression. No problem.

To set someone against somebody else means to persuade them that they have an enemy.
It was a sad and familiar story. His parents divorced when Orlando was young and he had to spend part of each week with his mother, and the weekends with his father. They each tried to set him against the other.
This verb always has the form SET one person AGAINST another.

set aside
Albert set ten percent of his salary aside every month. He was saving to get married.
Aside means 'to one side'. To have some money *set aside* means to have some money saved in a bank, put under the bed, or in a dirty old sock
put away, put aside, put by mean exactly the same.
Separable two-word verb . Be careful.

set back
When we change our clocks at the beginning or the end of summer, we set our clocks. We *set* them *forward* in the spring, and in the autumn we *set* them *back*.
Separable two-word verb Fixed expression.

set down

Like all phrasal verbs with set, *set down* has the idea of doing something that is inconvenient, difficult, or impossible to undo. You set something <u>down</u> when you don't expect it to get back up again.

When you set down wine in your cellar, you don't expect to drink it for a few years.

A taxi driver will set down his passengers at the airport. He doesn't expect to see them again.

<u>Separable two-word verb</u> . *Be careful.*

set forward

When we change our clocks at the beginning or the end of summer, we set our clocks. The direction in which time is going is <u>forward</u>. So we set them forward in the spring, and in the autumn we set them back.

<u>Separable two-word verbs</u>. *Fixed expression.*

set in

Sometimes, <u>in</u> has a rather vague meaning of 'around here, now' as opposed to <u>out</u> which can have the meaning of 'extension, away from here'

'The rain has set in for the day.'

This is common in England. This means that it is raining now, and it is going to be raining all day. There will be little change

<u>Two-word verb without an object</u> *No problem.*

set off

Here, off means 'from here', or 'from the situation here', like get off or take off
Set, as always, is difficult to reverse.

The Robertsons get in the car and set off (from the house) on holiday.

They expect not to come back for a quite a long time.
Set out means exactly the same.

Two-word verb without an object No problem.

set off

This is an explosive verb, a change of state off. When you set off a bomb, all the components and chemicals fly dramatically away from here. And it is definitely irreversible. Nobody has ever put a bomb back together again.

Separable two-word verb . Be very, very careful.

set on

Remember that *set* means, approximately, moving or changing something in such a way that it is difficult to move or change it back.

Well, Brian, why did the dog turn on you?
(On being aggressive here.) Probably that dog had a master, and that master did not like you at all. He set the dog on you. He ordered the dog to attack you.

Separable two-word verb. Fixed expression.

set out

Here, <u>out</u> means 'extension, away from here' as opposed to <u>in</u> which can have the meaning 'around here, about now'
Set, as always, is difficult to reverse.
Mr and Mrs Grant and all their children get in the car and set out (of the house) on holiday. They expect not to come back in a week or longer.
We say <u>set off</u> in exactly the same way.
<u>Two-word verb without an object</u> *No problem.*

set out

If you sell fish, at the beginning of the day you set out your fish on the counter, at the bar. You set your fish <u>out</u> on the counter.
<u>lay out</u> means the same here.
<u>Separable two-word verb</u> . *Be careful*

set up

I have just read about a very unusual nineteen-year-old. He has already set up five companies. He is a millionaire.
When you set something <u>up</u>, you erect it. You erect it in such a way that you hope that it doesn't fall over. By extension you *set up* a business. You start a business.
Criminals occasionally *set somebody up*, which means they arrange it so that the victim is set up as a target, either for the police or for other criminals.
Reggie spent ten years in prison for something he didn't do. He was set up by

the rest of his gang.
<u>Separable two-word verb</u>. *Be careful.*

settle
(settle, settled, settled)
When we settle, we have found the place we want to live in for the rest of our lives. Settlers were visitors to a land who intended to stay there and to farm the land. Settling is permanent.

settle for
<u>For</u> can mean 'in place of', or 'instead of'. <u>Take for</u> is a good example. Take one thing in place of another.
Igor wanted to be an astronaut, but he settled for flying business jets.

So when you settle for something, you have decided to accept something that is less than your dreams.
<u>Inseparable two-word verb</u> *No problem.*

show
(show, showed, shown)
To display or to demonstrate something, often as opposed to only talking about it.

show off
<u>Off</u> often has the sense of not being quite right. For example, <u>be off</u> and <u>go off</u>.
Show off means to display something, or

yourself, in a way that is not really acceptable. Often it means a vulgar display. Once, I saw a Rolls-Royce with all the metal parts covered in gold. Was this showing off?
Edwina was showing off her new car, so that we could admire it.
We use this verb with and without an object.
'Do you like Eddie's new car?'
'No. She is just showing off.'
<u>With an object, this is a separable two-word verb</u> Careful.

show up

We went out as a family for an evening meal, but Valerie and her husband didn't show up. We were worried because they didn't phone.
(That is, they didn't appear.)
Without an object, this is very similar to <u>turn up</u>.
Woody Allen says that an important part of success is *showing up*.
<u>Two-word verb without an object</u> No problem.

When you *show somebody up*, however, the meaning is very different. It means that you are *showing* that person - you are displaying or revealing him - <u>up</u> to the light of truth, up to the sight of the audience. You are revealing him to be a hypocrite. You are showing up the distance between his words and the truth.

He was a famous politician, a man of the

206

people, who lived simply. But then a reporter found his Swiss bank accounts, and showed him up.
<u>Separable two-word verb</u> . Careful.

shut
(shut, shut, shut)

When you shut the door, you cannot go in the room. Close the door means exactly the same. It is the opposite of open

shut up

<u>Up</u> is complete. Shut completely. Usually it means shut (your mouth) completely. It is a rude way of saying, *'Please, sir or madam, we have heard many of your words recently, and we were wondering if you could do us the favour of not speaking for a little while.'* Do not say this to anyone much larger or crazier than you.
Fixed expression.

sign
(sign, signed, signed)

To sign a letter or any other document is, of course, to put your name on it in your own handwriting. It means accepting responsibility for what is written there.

sign on

To *sign on*, in British English, means to accept the dole, the state money you get

when you have no job. In the good old days, unfortunate people had to sign <u>on</u> a cardboard form to receive their money.
<u>Two-word verb without an object</u> *No problem.*

sign up

<u>Up</u> is the direction of authority. When you *signed up*, you signed to defend the King against his enemies. You joined the army.
<u>Join up</u> has the same meaning, and to <u>be called up</u> means that you have been 'invited' to join the forces.
<u>Two-word verb without an object</u> *No problem.*

sink
(sink, sank, sunk)
What happens to a ship on the sea when it has a big hole. Think of the Titanic.

sink in

When you paint a dry wall, it takes time for the paint to sink into the surface. It takes time to sink <u>in</u>. We say this sometimes for new knowledge or new information. It can take a lot of time to *sink in*.

'The world has changed. The old ways will never come back.'
'I know. But it's hard to accept. It hasn't sunk in yet.'
<u>Two-word verb without an object</u> *No problem.*

sit
(sit, sat, sat)
What most people do on a chair.

sit down
<u>Down</u> reinforces the idea of *sit*. When we invite someone to a chair, we say, *'Sit down, please.'* We only say, *'Sit.'* to a dog.
Two-word verb without an object No problem.

sit up
Once somebody has *sat down*, we may suggest - especially if we are traditional teachers or in the army - that they *sit <u>up</u>*. That is, they sit with their backs straight, and that the person is concentrating and ready to listen.
Two-word verb without an object No problem.

sort
(sort, sorted, sorted)
To classify, which is something all people do all the time.

sort out
<u>Out</u> here is the end, the result. When you have sorted something out, you have finished the sorting, the problem is solved, and the annoyance has gone. Obviously we sort the good from the bad, the delicious from the poisonous, and so on. But the feeling of getting rid of something annoying

means that we can say *'sort out'* when no sorting has happened.
'Martha, didn't you tell me you had rats in your barn?'
'Yep, but the dog sorted them out.'
There are no more rats. The problem has gone. Good dog.
<u>Separable two-word verb</u> *Be careful.*

speak
(speak, spoke, spoken)
What we humans do when we have something to say.

speak out
When we *speak out* in the world, we speak publicly. If we protest the latest corruption scandal in our politicians, we speak out. There is always a sense of courage when someone speaks <u>out</u>, because it is always more comfortable - or even safer - not to say anything.
<u>Two-word verb without an object</u> *No problem.*

speak up
'Don't ever be shy in an English class,' said a good teacher. *'Speak up whenever you can.'*
If you tell me something in a quiet voice, maybe I can't hear you. I would then say to you, *'Speak <u>up</u>! I can't hear you.'* It means to speak louder, to raise your voice, to make yourself heard.

Compare this with turn up the radio.
Two-word verb without an object No problem.

split
(split, split, split)

To separate. Usually only into two parts. You split a log with an axe. A family can split into two adults who live apart, with children travelling to and fro.

split away

Split away means the same as break away. A group of unhappy politicians might split away from a political party. (You can also say that the group split off)
Two-word verb without an object No problem.

split off

Whereas break off is always hard (You can break something off with a hammer, perhaps.) *split off* can be soft like a cake mixture.You can split off half the sticky mixture to make a different kind of cake. The soft tentacles of some animals can split off.
Separable two-word verb Be careful.

split up

Up means completely. When a couple *splits up*, they are no longer a couple. They cannot split any more.

Two-word verb without an object No problem.

stand
(stand, stood, stood)
What we do on our feet when we do not move.

stand by
In space, <u>by</u> has the general idea of *'next to'* or *'close to'*
When you stand by someone, you stand next to them, you are ready to fight at their side. You are their ally.
And there are times when you have to *stand by* your words.
'Are you saying that the members of this committee are incompetent?'
'Yes. I stand by my words.'

In the military, you sometimes have to stand by your weapons. That means that the weapons are ready to use in a few seconds. By extension, when you are on duty but have nothing to do except to wait, you are *on stand-by*.
This is why modern machines with remote controls don't have *on* and *off* any more. They have *on* and *stand by*, which means they are ready to be turned on.

Inseparable two-word verb No problem.

stand for, run for
In Britain, when an ambitious person wants

to be a politician, he or she *stands for* election. In the United States, a would-be politician *runs for* election, which tells you something about the two different countries. For is why they are standing or running.
<u>Inseparable two-word verb</u> *No problem.*

stand for, stand up for

One of the commonest meanings of for is a purpose.
Eton, the most famous school in England, stands for a quality education. That is its purpose.
The red flag stood for Communism. That was a symbol.
NATO stands for North Atlantic Treaty Organisation. An acronym.

It can be moral as well.
Belinda resigned from the board of the company. She wouldn't stand for the deception being planned on the shareholders.
Note that in this sense, and only in this sense, you can use *stand up for* to add emphasis. You stand up, you are not on your knees.
Belinda wouldn't stand up for the deception being planned on the shareholders.
Bob Marley, the Reggie master, used to sing about standing up for your rights.
You can also *stand up for* other people. When you do this, you are supporting them

213

when they are attacked. When you stand up for somebody you also _stick up for_ them.
STAND FOR is an _inseparable two-word verb_ No problem.
STAND UP FOR is a _three-word verb_. No problem either.

stand in for

Sometimes in the theatre the star is ill. But the show must go on, so somebody else has to *stand in* the show *for* the star. She is the substitute. She *stands in for* the star. In fact, she is known as the *stand-in*.
Three-word verb. No problem.

stand out

Something or someone who *stands out* is easy to see, easy to pick out. Usually, with a person, we use this verb to mean that the person we are talking about *stands out* (from the crowd) because of excellence.
Two-word verb without an object No problem.
In fact 'outstanding' means 'truly excellent'.

stand up to

You are not on your knees, you are standing up
When you *stand up to* somebody, you have courage, you are not running away. You are standing and facing the enemy.
Three-word verb. No problem.

start

(start, started, started)
To begin (begin, began, begun). When you

start a project it is the very first thing you do in that project. If your project is to run a marathon, then you start by running ten metres. If you can do that, do another ten. And so on.

start out

Similar to <u>set out</u> in the sense of beginning a journey, but we usually mean on life's journey. We say this when we talk of a young man or woman, leaving school or home, setting <u>out</u> for the first time. They are *starting out*.
<u>Two-word verb without an object</u> *No problem.*

start up

<u>Up</u> can mean imagination and the courage to do something new. Even in hard times, there are always people who want to start up a business. Silicon Valley is full of *start-ups*. These are companies that famously *started up* in a garage.
<u>Separable two-word verb</u> *Be careful.*

stay
(stay, stayed, stayed)
To stay somewhere means to be somewhere for a considerable time.

stay ahead

In any race, the person, horse or car in front of the others, is ahead.

If you *stay ahead*, it means that you are *ahead* in the race, and that you continue to be ahead.

Keep ahead means exactly the same.
Two-word verb without an object No problem.

stay off

Off is the opposite of *on*, or it can be a move away from an *on* position.

'STAY OFF THE GRASS'

You might see this sign in a park. You are not on the grass, but don't go on it. Continue not to be on the grass.

'Keep off the grass' means exactly the same.
Inseparable two-word verb No problem.

stay out, stay out of

There is a sign at an electricity switching room.

'Danger of death. STAY OUT'

It means do not go in. You are out of the room, and you must continue to be out of the room.

Keep out means exactly the same.
STAY OUT is a *two-word verb without an object*

stay up

'Don't stay up for me, Mum. I won't be back till two.'

'Two in the morning? You're right. That's far too late for me to stay up. I need my sleep.'

Stay up late is what we do when we don't

want to - or can't - go to bed.
Two-word verb without an object No problem.

step
(step, stepped, stepped)

The horizontal parts of a staircase. You take a step on each step when you go up or down.

step down

When you step down, you take a step <u>down</u>. If you are in a high position, and you are caught 'borrowing' public money (depending in which country you are) you may have to step down. You might have to leave your job.

One day in the 1970s a British Prime Minister suddenly stepped down. We, the public, never <u>found out</u> why.
Two-word verb without an object No problem.

step up to

This is <u>up</u> to the limit. When you step up to the mark, you step so that your foot is exactly on the mark at the beginning of a race. You are ready to run, ready to compete, ready to win. You *step up to* the challenge, to the responsibility.
Three-word verb No problem.

stick
(stick, stuck, stuck)

When two things come together and it is

hard to separate them again, we say that they have stuck together. In the old days people stuck stamps to letters. When you drop your favourite ceramic teapot on the floor and it breaks into pieces, you can stick it together again.

stick at, stick to, stick with

These all mean the same.
To stick at something is a stronger way of saying keep at it.
Oh, Esmeralda. I know that you would rather go and out play with your friends, but you have to stick at your studies.
' Kids today! They can't stick to anything for more than ten minutes.'

However, *stick with* sometimes has another nuance. This is passive and is always unpleasant.
Noreen signed the contract without her lawyer there. Now she's stuck with it.
She can't escape from the contract. She can't get away.
<u>Inseparable two-word verb</u> *No problem.*

stick by

Similar to <u>stand by</u> but without the sense of strength or pride.
Your faithful dog, Fido the Mutt, sticks <u>by</u> you all day.
<u>Inseparable two-word verb</u> *No problem.*

stick up for
Very similar to stick up for but less dramatic.
'You're always sticking up for Milly. Why?'
'She's my friend, and you all have the wrong idea about her.'
Three-word verb No problem.

stick up to
Similar to stand up to but not as strong.
Three-word verb No problem.

take
(take, took, taken)
Everybody knows what *take* means. It is probably one of the first twenty words that a child learns. After *no*, and *mama*.

take after
'Mary has a bad temper. She is always angry. She takes after her uncle.'
Usually, after means later in time
Many years ago, perhaps, you took something after somebody else had them. You took your red hair after your grandfather.
The Smith boys are all slow at school. They take after their dad.
(He was slow at school as well.)
Take after always is to do with inheritance. You can compare this with name after.
Inseparable two-word verb No problem.

take away
When you go to a Chinese restaurant sometimes, instead of sitting down at a table, you can take the food back home with you. You can take it away. Away, as always, means that the restaurant will never see it again.
Separable two-word verb *Be careful.*

take back
Apart from the literal sense of taking a defective computer back to the shop, there is the idea that sometimes you have to take back your words. We all remember times when we have said something and found out that it was a mistake.
'And here are the photos of my family.'
'Who's this man?'
'My wife.'
Don't laugh too much. I know a man this happened to. Some words are very hard to take back.
Separable two-word verb *Be careful.*

take down
When an interesting teacher talks, you take the information down on to paper. You take notes.
Separable two-word verb . *Be careful.*

take for
When you *take* one thing *for* another, you mistake one for the other, you confuse two

things.

If you take toadstools for mushrooms and fry them for your dinner then that is the last mistake you will make.

<u>Separable two-word verb</u> *Always in the form TAKE X FOR Y.*

take from, take it from me

It's a fixed expression.*'Take it from me'*. It means that this is my opinion and I know what I am talking about.

take in

'Sue thought that Henry loved her, but she was taken in. He only wanted her for her money.'

If you tell a really good story, the audience is *taken into* the situation completely. We have all had the experience of being <u>in</u> the place that you can see in a film.

Telling a story is very, very similar to telling lies.

When you take someone in, you are lying and they believe you. You are deceiving them successfully.

Notice that in English we have to 'tell somebody something'. The person you are talking to must be mentioned, *except* in the expressions 'tell a story', 'tell lies', and 'tell the truth'. Notice that the truth is singular but lies often are not.

<u>Separable two-word verb</u> *but usually we use this verb in the passive.*

take off

Before the twentieth century it was incredibly difficult for humans to take themselves <u>off</u> the ground and into the air. But two American geniuses, called the Wright brothers, changed all that. In 1903 they made a machine that took itself off the ground with one of the brothers in it.

That machine, the world's first successful airplane, *took off* and later landed safely. And now, thousands of airplanes are taking off every hour

<u>Two-word verb without an object</u> *No problem.*

take on

When Don's mother died, his father didn't want to take on the care of his three children. So they all went to different homes.

As so often, <u>on</u> here means 'continuity' - think of <u>carry on</u> and <u>go on</u> - so if you take something on, it could be for a long time. Maybe it is a great responsibility, a heavy obligation. You *take <u>on</u>* a responsibility, a duty, an obligation.

Another common meaning is to take on somebody which means 'to employ them'. This is also a responsibility.

Mr Nightingale opened his new bar and so he took on ten people.

Notice the difference with <u>take up</u>, which is light. You *take up a hobby*, which you can drop any time.

<u>Separable two-word verb</u> . *Be careful.*

take out

Literally, to take something out implies 'take it out of this room' for example. You take the rubbish out for the dustman.

But, in the 60s in Vietnam, I think, this verb's meaning got a sinister new extension. To *take someone out* meant to take them out of the way, to kill them.
<u>Separable two-word verb</u> . *Be careful.*

take over

When his father retired, Mr Arbuthnot Jr took over the family business.

In any organisation, the people <u>over</u> you are the people in charge of you. To take charge means to take the responsibility. Take over means exactly the same thing.
<u>Separable two-word verb</u> . *Be careful.*

take to

I took to Beatrice the first time we met. We are really good friends now.

When we take to somebody, we take a liking to them. We like them, easily and quickly.
<u>Inseparable two-word verb</u> *No problem.*

take up

Don's wife is delighted. Since he took up gardening, he has not only lost ten kilos, but the garden is looking much better.

Where <u>take on</u> is heavy, Take up is light. It's easy to take things <u>up</u>. You can always put them down again. You take up a new hobby,

a new interest.
Separable two-word verb . *Be careful.*

take it up with
This <u>up</u> is talking to authority.
You have a problem with working ten hours a week for no extra? Take it up with your boss.
Separable three-word verb. *Unusual. Take note.*

talk
(talk, talked, talked)
What we humans do when we have something to say.
Talk is very similar to *speak*, but there is the sense of more words. In many expressions you can use both words.
Gemma's talking on the phone.
Gemma's speaking on the phone.
These mean exactly the same.
Gemma talks a lot.
Lots of words.
The main time we use *speak* and not *talk* is a language.
Charlie speaks good Russian.

talk around, talk round
To talk around the subject, to talk round the subject means to be indirect. *Cornelius wanted to marry Cornelia, but every day he found himself just talking <u>around</u> it*. He never got to the question, and Cornelia married someone else.
Inseparable two-word verb *No problem.*

talk back

After a verb, back almost always has the sense of *'return'*. For example, go back, think back, and so on. When a child *talks back* to his elders, it means that he is showing disrepect.
Inseparable two-word verb No problem.

talk down to

Some people do not have as much education, intelligence, money, beauty, or even experience of life as we have. Which means, in our opinion, that we are higher in some way than they are, so that when we talk to them, we have to talk down to them, or they will not understand.

Snobs, and people who love mirrors, do this all the time.

When somebody *talks down to* you, how do you feel? Me too.
Three-word verb. No problem.

talk over

It was an important family meeting and the whole family had to decide what to do with the farm. They talked it over for several days.

We often use over in the sense of 'from one side to the other'. For example, you turn over an omelette - turn it from one side to the other - when you are cooking it. Therefore *talk over* means 'to talk carefully

about something from every direction' before coming to a decision.
George asked Georgina to marry him She said they should talk it over.
Compare this with <u>think over</u>.
<u>Separable two-word verb</u> . Careful.

talk someone round

Talk someone round has a completely different meaning from <u>talk around something</u>. When you want to persuade somebody, usually it is better to be indirect. Perhaps you feel you have to talk around the subject first until your friend <u>comes round to</u> your way of thinking. Congratulations! You have *talked him round*. He now agrees with you.
<u>Separable two-word verb</u> Be careful.

tell

(tell, told, told. Like <u>sell</u>, sold, sold.)
Tell has at least three common meanings;
(1) It means 'say' in the sense of 'relate'.
We say something (to somebody), but we tell somebody something.
Mary says it is her birthday tomorrow.
Mary tells us it is her birthday tomorrow.
(These sentences mean exactly the same.)
With few exceptions *tell*, in this sense, **must** be followed by a person, and then the content.
The exceptions are -
tell stories

tell lies
tell the truth
which, if you think about it, are all very similar.

(2) When you *tell somebody to do something*, you are giving them an order, a command.

My boss told me to work harder.

(Notice how similar this is to '*My boss told me, "Work harder".*')

(3) *Tell the difference* to mean 'to distinguish'.

Bill and Ben are identical. Even people who know them can't tell the difference.

tell off

We often use <u>off</u> to mean being away from the target, or the intention, or what is right. When you *tell* somebody *off*, you are telling them what they are doing that is not right. You are not happy with them.

Teachers, parents, wives and husbands have been known to do this.

<u>Separable two-word verb</u> . *Careful*

think
(think, thought, thought)
What we do with our brains.

think about

To consider something.
'*What are you thinking about?*'
'*What to buy my father for Christmas.*'

Or to have an opinion
*'What do you think about Julio Iglesias?
'I think he's wonderful.'*
Grammar note. *Think about* in the sense of 'have an opinion' can never be in a continuous tense.
We have the best government that money can buy. Think about it.
Think of is similar to *think about*, but not exactly the same.
If we want to talk about thinking that takes time, we have to say *think about*.
Inseparable two-word verb   No problem.

think back

'Think back to when you were six years old,' said the psychiatrist. *'What do you remember?'*
Deliberately remember. After a verb, back almost always has the sense of 'return'
Two-word verb without an object   No problem.

think of

'Every time I hear that song, I think of my first boyfriend.'
'That is a very selfish man. He never thinks of other people."
When we use *think of* we can also use *think about*, but not the other way round. *Think about* is thinking carefully. It takes time.
Inseparable two-word verb   No problem.

think over

It was Leap Day, February 29th, and

Georgina asked George to marry her He said he would think it over..

This time, over means 'from one side to the other'. *Think it over* means 'to think carefully about something from every direction' before coming to a decision.
Compare this with talk over.
Think through has a similar meaning.
Separable two-word verb Careful.

think through

'Is this the right solution to your legal problems, Mr Bowen?'
'I don't know. I'll have to think it through.'
When you have a serious problem, if feels as if you are *in* it. And some problems we just have to think through. We have to think *through* the problem, and come up with a solution. It is a similar idea when we *get through* a lot of work. This means something much more deliberate than *think about* or *think of*.
Think over has a similar meaning, but more about the thinking. *Thinking through* means arriving at a conclusion. *Think of* Sherlock Holmes and his three-pipe problems.
Separable two-word verb . Careful.

think up

Mr O'Connor loved new technologies. He enjoyed seeing what designers could think up.

229

Sometimes in the old days we must have imagined that our minds lived in our stomachs. (Remember *bring up* in the sense of vomit.) Well, you can certainly *bring up* a new idea into the conversation.

Also, you can *think up* an idea. It means exactly the same as *come up with*.

Separable two-word verb . Be careful.

throw
(throw, threw, thrown)

What we do to stones, spears, balls, and so on when we want them a long way from us.

throw away

I like paper tissues. Use them, throw them away.

Away means you never see it again. To *throw it away* is to throw it into the rubbish, to discard it.

Mr Scharfstein went to Las Vegas, and threw all his money away.

Notice that if we are talking about throwing rubbish away from the house, we can also say throw out.

Separable two-word verb . Careful.

throw out

When you throw somebody out, you ask, or tell, (or force) that person to leave your house. Normally we do not literally throw them out of the door.

Sometimes we use this verb for things

instead of people. Then it means the same as throw away.
Separable two-word verb. Be careful.

throw up

Sometimes, unfortunately, the body has to throw unwanted food up out of the stomach. To *throw up* means 'to vomit'
Two-word verb without an object No problem

try
(try, tried, tried)

Try has two similar meanings that are not quite the same.

(1) The first meaning is *'to intend'* or *'to attempt'*. When we try to do something, we attempt to do it.
Arnold tried to get to school on time every day, but always there was a problem with the buses or the weather or something.
(2) The second meaning is closer to the idea of 'test'.
Beatrice tried drinking whisky, but she hated it. She won't touch it again.

Notice the grammar.
Try to do something = attempt to do it
Try doing something or *try something* = testing it

try for

For is usually the reason we do something.

'Do you think you will pass that exam?'
'I don't know, but I'm going to try for it.'
(I will make a good attempt.)
<u>Inseparable two-word verb</u> No problem.

try on

Try, here, has the second meaning of 'test'. (*Try* something = test it) When we buy clothes, we *try them <u>on</u>*. Do they fit well or not? Does the boyfriend or girlfriend approve or not?

By extension, when a naughty child wants to see how far he can go before being punished, she (or, more usually, he) will *try*, or test, his parents' patience. He will do something as bad as he dares so he can find out what will happen. He will trying it on.

'Why is Marcia screaming so much? I didn't touch her.'
'Don't worry about it. She's just trying it on. She does this all the time.'

Such a child is known as a very *trying* child.
<u>Separable two-word verb</u> . Be careful.

try out

Patricia from the Marketing Department has nine or ten new ideas every day. But when we try them out, it is always a disaster.

Try, here, has the second meaning of 'test'. (*Try* something = test it) Usually, we use this verb in the sense of testing an idea <u>out</u> in the real world to discover the final result.
<u>Separable two-word verb</u> . Be careful.

turn
(turn, turned, turned)
The basic idea of *turn* is rotate, revolve, go round in a circle. By extension, it can also mean a change of state. For example, when it is very hot, water turns to steam. Witches, they say, can turn princes into frogs.

turn about, turn around, turn round
These all mean the same. A big ship is very difficult to turn about. And a big company is also very difficult. You will often see this expression in the business press.
Hoo Boy Co. was losing money every year for ten years, until the new boss, Henry Makit, turned the company round.
<u>Separable two-word verbs</u>. *Be careful.*

turn against
Stephanie liked her local restaurant very much but she turned against it when she <u>found out</u> that the health department had discovered cockroaches in the kitchen. She never went there again.
<u>Against</u> always has the idea of 'confrontation'
When Pascual was a student, he was an ardent radical. Later in life, he turned against all his old beliefs. His friends accused him of <u>selling out.</u>
To *turn against* a person or an idea means

to reject them, after first accepting them.
Inseparable two-word verb *No problem.*

turn away

When you *turn* somebody *away* from your door, you do not let them in your house. You do not feed them, or entertain them. By extension, foolish people have been known to turn away opportunity when it arrives.
Separable two-word verb . Be careful.

turn down

Harry proposed to Harriet, but she turned him down.
(So he won't get married to her.)
A long, long time ago the Romans used to entertain themselves with watching fights to the death in the circuses. Traditionally, when a gladiator had won, he appealed to the crowd. The crowd would then decide whether to kill the defeated one or not by signalling with their thumbs. If they *turned* their thumbs *down*, he was killed.
To *turn something down* is to reject it.
When we *turn the music down*, we make it less loud. We make it quieter.
Compare this with turn on, turn off.
Separable two-word verb . Be careful.

turn in

Go to bed, go to sleep. Think of rolling into bed.
Two-word verb without an object *No problem.*

turn somebody in

Turn your enemy in to the police. Once you have *turned* him *in,* it could be a long time before he is out again. This means the same as *give him up.*
<u>Separable two-word verb</u>   Be careful.

turn into

The basic idea of *turn* is rotate, revolve, go round in a circle. You are happily driving your Rolls-Royce down the high street when suddenly you want to *turn into* a side street because you have just seen a place to park. Nice and simple. First you were in the busy high street, and now you are in a quiet road. You are in a different road, a different situation, perhaps, a different state.

By extension, when it is very cold, water *turns into* ice. It's a different situation, a different state.

When certain football supporters drink lots of beer, they can turn into hooligans.
<u>Inseparable two-word verb</u> No problem.

turn on, turn off

Years ago, radios were large brown things that usually had knobs, or rotating controls, that you had to <u>turn</u>. So, naturally, when you wanted to hear the news at six o'clock you turned <u>on</u> the radio. And when you finished the programme (US, program), you *turned it off*.

The technology has changed, of course, as it

always does. But we still turn on or turn off the TV, the computer, or anything else.

By extension, we use it to describe enthusiasm. If somebody seriously excites you, you could say that he or she *turns you on*.

The opposite is also true. A man who picks his nose in public will *turn off* most people. Put off can have the same meaning.

We can also say in this situation that Mr Nosepicker will *put people off*.

BE CAREFUL with turn on. To *turn someone on* means to seriously excite them, to get them enthusiastic, but to *turn on somebody* means to attack them. There is a difference.

Separable two-word verbs. Be careful.

turn on (somebody)

A dog could be looking somewhere else, and suddenly it turns *on* you. It turns and attacks you. Postmen and door-to-door salesmen know this well.

BE CAREFUL with this verb. It does not mean the same as *turn sombody on. Inseparable two-word verb* No problem.

turn out

Mary's husband seemed to be a nice man, but it turns out that he stole a lot of money from his last job.

That was the truth, the end result.

Turn, as in turn into, can mean change to a different situation, perhaps, a different

state, and _out_ is the final result. For example, _try out_, _carry out_, _die out_.
That is the final result. Whatever _turns out_ is the end, the result, the final truth.
Edmund's new business turned out fine. He's only 38, but he's going to retire.
<u>Inseparable two-word verb</u> No problem.

turn over

Literally, to turn over means what you do to a pancake, an omelette or a steak when you are cooking it. You turn it <u>over</u> from one side to the other.

In business, it describes the flow of money through a company. The money that comes in is the turnover, while the money left after all the expenses, is the profit. (If you need to know more, go and read an accountancy book.)

A big company, by definition, *turns over* lots and lots of money.
We use the noun TURNOVER more often than the verb.

turn to

When you *turn to someone*, you ask them for help, as opposed to <u>turn on them</u>.
<u>To</u> is often a more friendly preposition than <u>on</u> or <u>at</u>. Compare <u>come to</u> and <u>come at</u>.
<u>Inseparable two-word verb</u> No problem.

turn up

Years ago, people had far fewer forms of entertainment than now, and at night, in

candlelight, one of the most popular diversions was cards. When you turn <u>up</u> a card, it is always a surprise.
'Oh! Look what turned up. It's the Ace of Hearts.'
Therefore, when anything or anybody who turns up appears by chance, it is a surprise.
You'll never guess who turned up in the office. Georgie Bender. You remember him? It's been seven years since we last saw him.
<u>Two-word verb without an object</u> No problem.

turn (the music) up
When we *turn* the music <u>up</u>, we make it louder. We increase the volume.
<u>Separable two-word verb</u> . Careful.

use
(use, used, used)
What you do with a tool (usually) in your hands. I am using a computer to write this. Earlier I made some notes using a whiteboard and a few board pens. And teachers are always telling us to use our brains.

use up
This <u>up</u> means complete. When you *use it up*, there is none left.
We have used up all the wood for the barbecue, so we have to go home soon.
Doris lied so often that she has used up her credibility. Nobody now believes a word

she says.
<u>Separable two-word verb</u> Be careful.

watch
(watch, watched, watched)

To look closely, to observe. If a man says to his friend in the street, 'Hey, look at that lady.' his friend will look for a second or two and may well say something. But if the man tells his friend to watch the lady, his friend will spend some time to observe her. He will try to <u>*find out*</u> what she is doing.

watch for, watch out for

Watch for does not mean the same as <u>*look for*</u>.

The gallant knight Sir Julian de Flor went into the forest to look for treasure, but he had to watch for dragons.

Watch for, watch out for means to stay alert and observant. There are dangers everywhere.

But notice that *watch out for* is the same as <u>*look out for*</u>.

<u>Inseparable two-word verb</u> No problem.

watch out

Watch out means almost the same as <u>*look out*</u>, but whereas *look out* can be a scream meaning danger **NOW!** *watch out* is normally a warning of a possible danger in the future.

*'You're going to Slum City tonight? I'd

watch out if I were you.'
<u>Two-word verb without an object</u> No problem.

watch over

This is watching from high up *over* what you see. When you *watch over* something you look carefully over it, you observe it continuously. So you are guarding it. Mama watches over the baby, and the foreman watches over the factory floor.
<u>Inseparable two-word verb</u> No problem.

wear
(wear, wore, worn)

We *wear* jackets, skirts, trousers, and shoes. We also wear glasses, rings, and watches, but we *carry* suitcases and shopping bags. In other words, if it is attached to our bodies, we wear it.

wear in

Certain pop stars used to pay assistants to wear in their new shoes for them

New clothes - new shoes in particular - can be very stiff and uncomfortable. They have to be *worn* for some time before we are happy with them. They have to be *in* use for a while. They have to be *worn in*.
<u>Separable two-word verb</u> . Careful.

wear out

When we have worn clothes for a long time, they go out of shape, holes appear, the colours fade, and so on. They become *worn out* and we throw away our old shirts or give them to charity. They go *out* of use. They are finished.

'I never buy cheap clothes,' said Steve. 'They wear out too fast.'

By extension, we also say this of machines, and then we throw them away as well.

Sammy would have to buy a new bike every couple of years. He was always wearing them out.

We also say when someone is really tired, that they are *worn out*.

Shoes WEAR OUT. Two-word verb without an object No problem.
We WEAR them OUT. Separable two-word verb .

work
(work, worked, worked)

Work means what you do every day to get food on the table and a new Mercedes in the garage. It also means *'to function'* as in *'my new Mercedes works very well.'*

work off

To *work off* a debt means that you must work to pay the debt, and to work *off* a few kilos means that you feel too fat and you are going to the gym to suffer.

You can't afford to pay for that lovely meal you have just eaten in the restaurant? No problem. You can *work it off*. We need

somebody to wash the dishes in the kitchen. You'll only have to work for seventeen hours.
Every New Year, Anna goes to the gym to work off the extra weight of Christmas.
<u>Separable two-word verb</u> . Be careful.

work on
Dora doesn't want to go out for the next few weeks. She is working on her thesis.
You work <u>on</u> a project.
<u>Inseparable two-word verb</u> No problem.

work out
You have a problem in your mind, and it is worrying you. You cannot get to sleep, and your daily life has become more difficult. The problem is *in* your mind. Then, suddenly, AHA! You have the solution. You can now do something <u>out</u> in the real world. The problem has been worked out. It has been solved.
Grandpa says that he didn't have calculators when he was a child. He had to work everything out in his head.
<u>Separable two-word verb</u> . Be careful.

<u>Out</u> can be the final result, such as <u>try out</u> or <u>die out</u>.
'Hi, Jim. What happened to that legal case with your uncle's will?'
'Fine, Harry. It worked out fine. Want some champagne?'
The final result was fine for Jim.

In this sense, it is a two-word verb without an object No problem.

Work out is a newer expression. *Work* (your stress, your problems, or even your fat) *out* (of your body). It means 'to exercise a lot in a gym until you can hardly walk home.'
After a week in the tax office, Peter loves working out in the gym. He sleeps very well on Friday nights.
In this sense as well, this is a two-word verb without an object No problem.

work round to

If you have a lot of work, maybe it takes time to *work round to* everything. We more often use *get round to* with the same meaning.
Three-word verb No problem.

243

Printed in Great Britain
by Amazon.co.uk, Ltd.,
Marston Gate.